Castles
IN THE AIR

JUDY CORBETT

EBURY
PRESS

This edition published in 2005

First published in Great Britain in 2004

10 9 8 7 6 5 4 3

First published by
Ebury Press
Random House
20 Vauxhall Bridge Road
London SW1 2SA

Random House Australia (Pty) Limited
20 Alfred Street, Milsons Point
Sydney
New South Wales 2061, Australia

Random House New Zealand Limited
18 Poland Road, Glenfield, Auckland 10
New Zealand

Random House South Africa (Pty) Limited
Endulini, 5A Jubilee Road
Parktown 2193
South Africa

Random House UK Limited Reg. No. 954009

www.randomhouse.co.uk

A CIP catalogue record for this book is available from the British Library

ISBN 0 091 89731 9

Typeset by Textype, Cambridge
Printed and bound in the UK by Cox & Wyman Ltd, Reading, Berkshire

For Peter

PLAN:

A   GATEWAY

B   GATE HOUSE

C   SOLAR TOWER

D   HALL OF JUSTICE
    (GHOST ROOM ABOVE)

E   DINING ROOM

F   HALL OF MEREDITH
    (FIRST FLOOR)

G   KITCHEN

H   DUKE OF BEAUFORT'S CHAMBER
    (FIRST FLOOR)

I   "JACOBEAN ROOM"
    (KING'S ROOM ABOVE)

J   KNOT GARDEN

K   SIR JOHN'S ARCH

L   COACH HOUSE

M   THE OLD DUTCH GARDEN

N   THE GREAT TERRACE

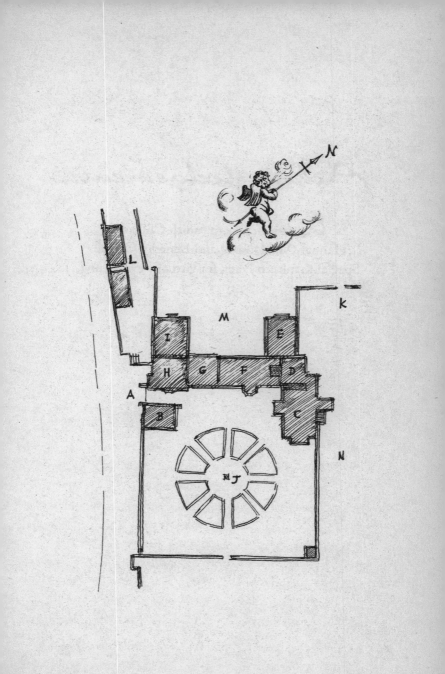

Acknowledgements

With thanks to Judith Chilcote,
Hannah MacDonald and Lenedra Carroll.
Special thanks to Peter, for virtually everything.

Contents

Prologue

I have just had to dry the sheets with a hairdrier again before getting back into bed. I left our two lurcher dogs bundled up in the blankets hoping they would keep the bed aired a bit; but it's no good, everything is damp again. I can cope with the damp if it's warm damp; it's the cold damp that defeats me. I also found two woodlice in the bed which I blasted out with the hairdrier. It's been a long night, almost not worth going back to bed, but the cold is a very good reason to burrow back beneath the blankets.

My husband, Peter, is still out there in the dark passageway emptying rainwater from innumerable buckets. My areas of duty are the Hall of Meredith, the west wing and the Royal Bedroom. It is four thirty in the morning and in total we will have emptied sixteen buckets: but the situation is improving. In the beginning we used to empty thirty-six buckets between us. I say buckets, but in fact there is an eclectic assortment of vessels (anything from seed trays to casserole pots) scattered across the floors of the castle which catch the drips from our leaking roof. Certain drips can be awkward to catch, especially the ones that roll down the walls and this is the type we have most of. It requires a vessel that will allow itself to be squashed up tightly against the wall and we have found that washing-up bowls with the rims cut off are the best type of receptacle for the job. When it's very dark in the castle and the batteries have run out in the torch and I can't find a dry match to light a candle, the symphony of drips guides me through the rooms. I have learnt to distinguish a coal scuttle from a paint pot and know exactly where I am by the tone of the drip. Once, some do-gooder rearranged my buckets and that left me floundering in the dark having to feel my way round the walls.

This is the darkest place I have ever known. Wonderfully, there is no light pollution and if there are no stars or a moon it can seem lighter if you close your eyes. The darkness laps around you like a great invisible sea; you fall into it and it closes, softly, over your face. Blindfolded by darkness, my fingers have learnt to read the crevices in the walls like Braille.

On these night-time manoeuvres around the house I have taken to wearing Peter's dressing gown with wellingtons and a bobble-hat which my mother gave me. He says he can always tell where I am because of the sound of my wellingtons slapping the backs of my legs, which apparently sounds like wet fish hitting a marble slab. Since I have stolen his dressing gown for its fleecy lining, he has taken to wearing a T-shirt, a tweed jacket and wellingtons. The draughts must be cold on his legs but at least we look equally ridiculous, which can be a comfort at times.

The rain is driving hard against the windows again. Because this side of the house faces north it gets quite a battering from the wind and rain. None of the windows fit in our bedroom because the stone mullions were replaced by cheap wooden frames after the fire of 1922. Consequently, rain blows in through the gap between frame and wall. The window sills are hopeless places for storage. I've got tons of soggy books because of them. Now I understand the stealth of water and how insistent it can be, I don't take any chances.

We are living in the one wing that has some semblance of a roof, but even that is minimal. In the beginning we had no hot water, no heating and very little electricity. It felt like an endurance test which took a great deal of determination to cope with in the very cold, wet weather. Hot water is the greatest luxury; it's marvellous for unfreezing toes in the winter, though it's very bad for chilblains. But when I think of the adventures and the joy this house has given us, even under these conditions, I can forgive it anything.

We bought Gwydir Castle in North Wales almost five years ago to the day. How extraordinary that sounds. We actually own Gwydir Castle! I still have to keep telling myself this because it hasn't quite sunk in yet, which is strange after all we've been through. Peter was twenty-nine and I was twenty-six. We weren't married then. It seems like a kind of miracle that we are still here and there really are elements of the fairy tale to our story. On paper the odds look fairly stacked against us being here at all: firstly, the castle wasn't on the open market; secondly, it was full of squatters (though they wouldn't thank me for calling them that); thirdly, we had a cottage-sized budget; and fourthly, the castle was little more than a crumbling ruin by modern standards, and certainly not fit for human habitation.

The house, which was described in some old sale particulars I found recently as 'one of the best-known Seats in the Country', came with a gatehouse, a coach house (both derelict), ten acres of wilderness which had once been a formal garden, twenty peacocks and Sven. Dear Sven. I was just thinking about him as I came back to bed.

I hope this rain isn't finding its way into his old caravan. He used to live up by the log shed at the back of the house, in an area which has become known as Upper Svenham. He was here when we bought the house and for a long time came in every day for a hot meal and a wash. He was about fifty then, very mean-looking on account of his broken nose and stubble-covered head, but his looks very definitely belied the inner man in that regard. His broad Liverpudlian accent made communication very difficult indeed and we were forced to adopt a form of sign language which allowed for limited conversation. I have tried many times to think up a fair job description for him: groundsman implies that we have fine lawns and neat borders to maintain, which we don't (ours is more chainsaw gardening at present); odd-job man sounds too menial, so I shall opt for the middle way and say handyman, though a less handier man with tools and machinery I have yet to meet. Sven toiled in the garden.

Gwydir is 'partly ruinous and inhabited by poor persons', wrote the Reverend W. Bingley in 1800. Nothing much has changed in that regard. On my way down to the kitchen earlier, I tried to remember how the house looked when we first moved in. It gets harder and harder the more things we do to improve the state of the rooms. The mess was split between romantic mess and sordid mess. The romantic mess revolved around what nature had been allowed to do in the uninhabited parts of the house, such as the ivy cascading in through the little leaded windowpanes which bathed the rooms in an eerie green light, and the Virginia creeper which poured in through the roofless parts of the house. The sordid mess entailed what the previous occupants had done to it: the bar, the swirling carpets, the flimsy partitions, the stale stench of beer and cigarettes and municipal disinfectant. To the previous occupants it was nothing more than a funky place to have a party. To me, it was the incarnation of a childhood fantasy.

Most of the castle dates back to the beginning of the sixteenth century, but the two stair towers are much earlier and are said to have come from a nearby abbey during the Dissolution of the Monasteries. A substantial portion of the house was demolished circa 1819 by Lord Willoughby d'Eresby but the oldest parts remain. Further wings were added in the 1550s and 1828. It is my very favourite kind of house where all the different periods have been kneaded together by the passage of time into one harmonious chain of limestone walls and plum-coloured roofs.

The wing we sleep in had a very nasty makeover sometime during the late 1960s (1969 according to Peter, who likes to be specific about dates) when the worst style of interior decoration was in vogue. There were French windows and patio doors leading out into a wilderness that was once a garden. The bathroom had pink fittings, pink walls and brown and cream tiles, and the downstairs looked like the inside of a very sleazy nightclub, which indeed it was before we bought the castle. There was even a 'Ladies' and 'Gents', complete with malodorous urinals and an Expelair, which had been punched through the leaded lights of an original sixteenth-century window.

So much has happened since we first moved in. I know the house so well now it could almost be an extension of my own body. It lives in me as much as I live in it. I know every sound it makes, every squeal of every door. I know how each window needs to be shut – some slammed hard, others eased back into their frames. I know how to journey across the house without making a floorboard creak.

1
Finding the Castle

$\mathcal{W}$e found the castle on a warm afternoon in late spring. Peter and I had spent a lazy day in Llanrwst, which was then to us an anonymous little market town about fifteen miles south of Conwy, in the heart of northern Wales. The distant mountains were streaked with white where a late snow had gathered in the contours of the slopes: Cnicht, the Carnedds, the Glyders, and mighty Snowdon itself, Yr Wyddfa in Welsh, which towered eagle-spans above the others.

Ostensibly we were house-hunting, but a town with an antique shop and a good parish church always delayed us. There were lines of very shabby bunting criss-crossing the streets which appeared to have been hanging there since the previous summer. A string of home-grown shops lined the narrow streets, a few boarded up with FOR SALE signs in their windows and leaves banking the doorways, but mostly the town still retained a gentle pre-war atmosphere.

We found the parish church of St Grwst on the banks of the River Conwy. We arrived on the hour as a bell chimed from a stone tower. The door to a side chapel was open. We slipped in and were engulfed by the smell and the atmosphere of the past. Inside, the cool, green flagstones were dappled with squares of light from the leaded windowpanes. There was dust on the mouldings of the wooden panelling and a strong smell of candle grease; it was a balm to the senses. The past was a refuge where we both hid from the rigours of the modern world. Peter's enthusiasm for history was boundless. He had a way of speaking of the distant past as though it were yesterday.

My interest was more instinctive, less academic. It was simply that I felt more comfortable with the dead than I did with the living.

There was Llewelyn the Great's sarcophagus conspicuously resting in the shado̶s. The massive stone chest which had once held the body of the great Welsh prince now held only spiders. The walls of the chapel were covered with memorial brasses to the Wynn family: 'Heere Lyeth The Body of Sr J̶̶n Wynne of Gwydir Kt And Baronet who Died Ye F̶̶ of ̶̶ 1626.' A tablet erected to the memory of h̶̶ also caught my eye with its enigma̶̶ ̶̶ PUMUS, FUMUS, FUIMUS, ECCE' ̶̶ A reality is a vapour. We have been. Behol̶̶

C̶̶ to a helpful churchwarden, was t̶̶ ̶̶ of the Wynn's was called Gwydir Cas̶̶ ̶̶ ̶̶ and when ̶̶ ̶̶ beyond the thick walls o̶̶ ̶̶ ks.

A memory s̶̶ ̶̶ cocks at Gwydir Castle but n̶̶ ere. I must have been no more than ̶̶ collections of the day had been overshadow̶̶ ̶̶ uma of finding my hand resting next to the sleeping ̶̶y of an adder, on a wall in nearby Betws-y-Coed.

Usually, the only way I could persuade Peter out of an historic building was by offering to take him to another. The use of this tactic meant we would sometimes spend whole days plodding around a string of historic sites, which could include anything from a grand country house to a prehistoric burial chamber. After spending two hours scrutinising every possible iconographic detail of the late medieval rood screen in the church, I suggested we visit Gwydir Castle. His eyes lit up. We left the churchwarden polishing the brass candlesticks on the altar.

We harboured a dream of one day buying a ruinous old mansion and renovating it as accurately as possible and living in it without electricity or any concessions to modern life. My dream was to wear a chatelaine round my waist, and keep wolfhounds and tend bees in some quiet corner of a walled garden. I had a strong sense of the Gothic in me, and neglected houses, in particular, appealed to something deep within my psyche. Peter said he would be happy to fall in with anything, provided the house was pre-1670 and had held Royalist allegiance during the Civil War; living in a Parliamentarian house was out of the question. My mother said we had 'allusions'. I'd lost count of how many times we'd trudged across water-logged fields to see crumbling old farmhouses with trees growing out of the chimneys. We were skilled in the art of trespass and had learnt to judge the amount of real menace in a collie dog's bark. The whole thing was a pipe dream really but the fantasy kept us sane. Without proper jobs or a steady income, buying somewhere seemed an unlikely eventuality. Peter had trained as an architectural historian at the Courtauld Institute in London and I had trained as a bookbinder at the London College of Printing. Neither profession was likely to make our fortune or fund the megalomaniac restoration schemes we fantasised about.

When I was younger, growing up on a hill farm in North Wales, I forged stronger bonds with houses than I did with people. Houses were secure, reliable; they provided unconditional sanctuary from a world I didn't quite fit into. The landscape of my childhood was littered with abandoned farmhouses. Often the families had just walked out and left all their belongings behind. I wondered what could have happened that would make a family abandon their past in such an abrupt way. These were solitary, lonely places. One in particular stays with me. It was an old stone farmhouse built into the side of a hill, surrounded by gorse bushes and mossy walls that the sun never reached. A grass path led up to a small cast-iron gate that had subsided gracefully into a patch of nettles. No sheepdog barked on the end of a chain. The chimneys loured without the benign presence of smoke to soften them. Pushing open the warped front door with its peeling paint, I was gripped by that old familiar fear of the unknown. I held my breath in expectation of the warty hag I knew must come lurching towards me. But the blackness remained quiescent and I forced myself to step across the threshold knowing instinctively that if I could conquer my fear here, alone on the side of this mountain, somehow life would be a little less troubling in the long run. Once inside, it was an altogether different proposition. I was enfolded in a world of secrets and the quiet whisperings of the past. There was nothing to be afraid of. The little parlour was as it had been the day the family left, except that nature had crowded in on the scene. An old Welsh bible lay open on the table, now smeared with swallow droppings; the table was laid for tea with dusty blue and white china cups and plates; there was even a jar with a hard nugget of fossilised jam inside. Ivy entwined itself lovingly around the turned banisters like a silk scarf encircling a pale throat. These scenes of quiet dilapidation frothed through my hungry imagination like an overfilled glass. It was here I was happiest, abstracting the self in this landscape of dreams.

When I was very small I used to visit the house of a neighbour and friend. On the stairs of her house were a series of sepia photographs in two large burr-walnut frames. They were of a large, romantic country house that had beautiful gardens and sweeping lawns. It was archetypal in some undefined way. It was redolent of threadbare tapestries and suits of armour. There was something about the cloistered atmosphere of this house that made me carry those images right through my teenage years. I would go there in my mind when the real world deserted me. If I had a choice (though the possibility of choice did not register as a likelihood then) this was the house I would spend the rest of my days living in.

'Wales? Why Wales,' asked our friends (with an eye to the weekend break) when they heard we were looking for a house to restore. 'Why not Andalucia or, even better, Tuscany?' Put simply, we didn't want to live abroad. Notions of deserting sinking ships came to mind, but more profoundly I happened to love Wales. *Hiraeth*, the Welsh word for homesickness, has become a cliché now, but I felt it so strongly when I lived in London; that strange and acute yearning of the heart for the place of one's birth. It was the old Wales I loved, not the Wales of the tourist: of ladies in stovepipe hats and railway stations with unpronounceable names; but the Wales of the *Mabinogion*, and the poet-bards, Dafydd ap Gwilym and Iolo Goch. I loved rain, mountains and Dylan Thomas – what better reasons for wanting to live in Wales? And despite the Act of Union in 1536, Wales had managed to cling on to its own language – a kind of miracle when one considers the logistics of such a thing. I may have been born and brought up in Wales but I didn't speak the language, so there was plenty of scope for feeling like a foreigner in my own country – there just wouldn't be any sun or olives.

Every weekend we would race up the M40 back to North Wales where my mother still lived, and I would feel like a salmon fighting its way upstream to the place of its birth. Peter, too, had been infected by this deep love of Wales, by its wild, moody beauty and ancient heritage. He longed to get out of London and nurture his own dream of one day becoming a full-time artist. The modern world bewildered us. Wales provided us both with a mechanism for escape. Peter, in particular, sought refuge in the past of the seventeenth century. His knowledge and under-standing of the period was prodigious, his passion for it often eerie in its acuteness. There were large areas of Wales that were still unspoilt; and where modern man treads least there is a stronger contact to be made with the past.

Every weekend, armed with the appropriate 'Royal Commission on Ancient & Historic Monuments' volume, we would take an area on the OS map and comb it thoroughly for ancient, derelict houses. We covered everything from sheepfolds to mental hospitals. It was staggering how many really important Welsh houses had been pulled down since the 1950s. Sometimes it felt as though we had lived under the worst excesses of a Stalinist regime. By the early '90s the demolition had virtually ceased, but change of another kind continued as the craze for double-glazing and pebbledash carried on the wind like a plague to the remotest spots.

We once returned together to that farmhouse of my childhood. A four-wheel-drive jeep stood in the newly tarmacked driveway and a satellite dish covered the 1741 date stone. The swallows had left and a Dobermann eyed us over the garden wall. I felt physical pain when I saw what had been done to that house. It was like meeting an old friend who was suffering from total amnesia, who couldn't now remember me. Peter led me away past the stumps of two felled oak trees as though from a graveside. For people who cared about the look of things, this was a difficult age to be living in.

After that we decided to penetrate deeper into the wilder parts of the country, further away from the urban tremors of Manchester and Liverpool. We saw some haunting sights. Often the old country house had disappeared altogether; an overgrown drive lined with ponticum, or a flight of garden steps to nowhere. Sometimes there would be more poignant reminders: a pile of old stones, a shoe, a book, or a lead water hopper poking out of the rank grass. We spent five years searching for an unspoilt derelict house, but the ones we liked the most were never for sale and even if they had been, we could never have afforded them. Most farmers had very inflated ideas of what their Tudor hall house, now a ruinous pig shed, might be worth.

As students we spent what little money we had buying early oak furniture in anticipation of the great house we would one day own. For those with a little specialist knowledge there were still bargains to be had in the junk shops of London. It took time and perseverance. Our rented accommodation bulged with Jacobean chairs and coffers, candlesticks and carvings. But perhaps our most eccentric purchase was 2,500 square feet of Jacobean small-field panelling which we stored in my mother's garage for five years. She was very patient. What on earth did we want with 2,500 square feet of oak panelling? she had asked. Good question. Neither of us were sure at the time but we had a feeling that one day it might just come in useful.

As we drove out of the town towards the castle the sun broke through the clouds. There was an awesome grandeur to the scenery. High up, on the valley slopes, the sunlight caught the limestone crags which pushed out through a dense canopy of spruce trees. We crossed the River Conwy by way of a narrow stone bridge that bore the date 1636. The white blossoms on the horse chestnuts stood erect like candles on a German Christmas tree. We looked to our left across a bald field of sheep-cropped grass and saw a flash of stone peeping out of the trees. There was nothing to match the excitement of catching that first glimpse of an interesting old house. We wound down the windows to try to get a better look, and then suddenly, there it was – not so much a castle but a large stone mansion nestling at the base of a massive, peninsula-like crag. It kept disappearing and re-emerging between the trees: soaring chimneys and mullioned windows, and a tall, narrow tower with a row of little arched windows running down its front like buttons on a coat. Perched on a rock, elevated a little above the castle, was Gwydir Uchaf, once the summer house of the Wynn family, the dynasty that had ruled the Conwy Valley since the fifteenth century. Next to it I could just make out the east window of a tiny stone chapel.

We took a left turn, skirting a broken-down wall, hoping to find the entrance, and a little further along, as the road doubled back on itself, we came across a weathered old gateway banked with leaves. There were two stone lions with shields on either side of two massive oak gates flanked by the initials IW and the date 1555, which, Peter told me, stood for Iohannes Wynn (Iohannes being the Latin for John). The sandstone was crumbling like a good Lancashire cheese and weeds sprouted in the mortared joints. A rotting rope dangled from a bell which creaked eerily in the thin breeze. Further along the road we found a shabby farm gate and a home-made sign which said 'Gwydir Castle – Coach Parties Welcome'. My heart sank when I saw that sign. It conjured up images of fake stocks and mock medieval jousting tournaments – everything in fact that represented the lower end of the 'fast-food' heritage industry. It did not bode well for Gwydir.

After the tantalising glimpse we had had of the castle, trespass was inevitable. With the agile skill of Russian gymnasts, we were up and over the gate and into the garden in moments. All around, the lawns had reverted to ragwort and thistle and the laurel hedges were bolting for the blue sky. It was like another world within the confines of those high stone walls. We patted the huge girth of a fine cedar of Lebanon. A sign nailed to its trunk said 'This tree is one of twelve cedars planted in 1625 in honour of Charles I's wedding'.

An arch at the end of a narrow path beckoned us forward. Carved into the spandrels were a lion and an eagle, their foreheads troubled by frowns. A wall of tangled foliage kept the house hidden until the very last moment when we ducked under the archway into a large courtyard. Peter and I stood speechless. It was a moment of profound revelation to me. It was the house in the sepia photographs, the memory of which I'd carried around all these years. It was the dream incarnate.

I felt like some medieval pilgrim come in from the desert happening upon some ancient and glittering city for the first time. In all our searching I had never seen such a beautiful place.

The house was almost completely hidden under swathes of wisteria and ivy. The pale afternoon light picked out the sandstone mullions around each window and made the little leaded panes glint randomly like the blocking of a crossword puzzle. The house seemed always to have been there. It was as though the mountains had grown up around it. A line of white doves flew out of an upstairs window and encircled the house. A forest of weeds and small holly trees grew out of the top of each chimney stack. Squares of thick black plastic covered holes in the roof and many of the windows were smashed. It looked empty of life and abandoned. An inquisitive peacock eyed us from the wall.

It didn't appear, at first glance, to conform to any building type I had seen before. It looked like several houses all tacked together as one. The hall range which faced us was low and long, collegiate almost, like an Oxford college or an abbey, and pinned to its front was a little stone stair tower with arched Gothic windows, which together with the ivy gave the house an otherworldly, *Morte d'Arthur* look. It was as though someone had baked a house to meet our requirements: a bit of late medieval and Tudor for Peter, a bit of nineteenth-century Gothick for me. The hall range was attached at the corner, at right angles, to an immense square tower, the Solar Tower, which rose to four storeys and looked rather daunting and keep-like in comparison. It had a lofty porch glued to its front and a tattered Welsh flag hanging from a drooping pole gave it the air of a house deserted by its garrison.

We found we were standing in some kind of box-hedge parterre. Amidst a wilderness of scutch grass and buttercups we could just make out a knot garden planted in the shape of a Tudor rose. In the centre, marooned in a sea of weed-infested gravel, was a stone column, naked without its sundial. The sad cry of the peacocks echoed around the courtyard.

We knocked at an oak door studded with rusty nails. Nobody came. We knocked again. Still no movement from within. The house seemed asleep beneath its wrapping of foliage; silent and waiting. We tried the handle and to our surprise the door opened, squeaking marvellously on unoiled hinges. It took a moment for our eyes to adjust to the darkness. The windows were veiled by undergrowth, but in the green and mysterious light we could see the detritus of a recent party: crunched beer cans, streamers, crumpled serviettes, smashed glasses strewn across the flagstones. Although a fire smouldered in a huge fireplace, the house appeared to be empty. This was our chance to see the house – if we hovered tentatively on the threshold we might never get the opportunity again. We stepped down onto the sweating flagstones and were engulfed by the gloom and an overwhelming smell of municipal disinfectant and mushrooms.

What immediately struck us as we crept silently around the house was that the Victorians, or someone later, had done their worst to the interior. Every last vestige of plaster had been hacked from the walls and only a fragment of panelling remained in an upstairs passageway. Every room had been thoroughly picked over, stripped of everything that might conceivably have a value. Most of the inglenook fireplaces had been stripped back to the beam and then infilled with 1940s grates. In some rooms electric trunking zigzagged the walls and smoke alarms dangled from the ceilings. But in spite of the modern disfigurements – and there were many – the sense of the past was almost tangible. It hung on the air like incense. It was redolent of heavy velvet drapes, candle wax and cobwebs. And it was eerie. Never before in my life had I felt so embraced by the past.

The central hall range was the most intact. Climbing up the spiral staircase, our feet cradled in the worn-out hollows of the steps, we emerged into a vast hall where ancient, blackened timbers supported the roof. The view from the mullioned windows, out across the neglected garden to the conifer-cloaked mountain beyond, was breathtaking. The avenue of twenty-two yew trees harboured the ghosts of topiaried shapes and there were vestiges of old terraces in the slope leading down to a weed-filled fountain basin. From this elevated position we could see that the bones of the old garden were still there, like the cheekbones of a beautiful face; but nature had been given its head and the lawns had become a rippling wilderness of buttercups. There was a pony grazing in the lower garden and some chickens were scratching around at the base of a yew tree. It was a wild place now.

Like sleepwalkers we wandered on down dark passageways where treacherous floorboards threatened to give way beneath our feet. One room which had 'Danger' chalked on the door was full of rotting carpets and sodden mattresses, and looking up you could see grey sky peeping through the holes in the roof. Someone had daubed their initials across the floorboards and up on the roof timbers. I wondered who DWR and EMER were and what had provoked them to leave their signature on the house, like tomcats marking their territory. In places, ivy crawled up through the floorboards and anaemic-looking mushrooms grew out of the walls. There were doves roosting in the Great Chamber. The yardstick by which I measured the suitability of any potential house was whether I could imagine myself reading in it. Gwydir was unquestionably a reader's house: there were window seats and dreamy views and, most importantly, apart from the peacocks, there was absolute silence.

I was so saddened that such a venerable old house had been brought to its knees in this way. I wanted to wrap my arms around it and comfort it as you would a small child. The more I saw, the angrier I became, angry with the people and the authorities who had allowed this to happen. And with that anger came another, fiercer emotion which took me completely by surprise. I knew as I ran my fingers over the damaged walls and as I picked up the broken shards of stained glass which lay scattered across the floorboards, that I would be prepared to do anything to save this house. I knew Peter felt the same. Maybe, just maybe, the owners, whoever they were, might be prepared to sell the house to us. They clearly didn't value it, so why not? It was such an extraordinary notion, I laughed out loud. 'Calm down and be rational,' I told myself. 'No, no, don't be rational,' an inner voice said, 'grasp the nettle.' Peter and I both knew, as we had never known anything before in our lives, that we had found the house of our most irresponsible dreams.

2
First Catch Your Hare

I am sitting up in bed now with my notebook resting against my knees and I am tolerably warm. The dogs have taken Peter's place by my side and their legs appear to be taking up about two-thirds of all the available bed space. Still, it is a great comfort to have their warm, breathing bodies next to me.

The bed we sleep in is a bit rickety. We made it ourselves about a year ago and it is already beginning to show signs of homemadeness. It is a four-poster in the most literal sense, in that it consists of four fence posts and a mattress. I have been meaning to dress it with velvet for months if only to chasten it a little, but somehow our comfort always comes last on the list of priorities. The rain is continuing to batter the windows and there is no great incentive to get up just yet, so I will allow myself a few more moments of warmth before I throw myself into the day.

I have to work very hard to make my mind go back to the early days. My memory is always a bit reluctant to call up something which gave it trouble at the time. But go back to it I must, if I am to give an accurate picture of how we came to be at Gwydir.

The castle was owned, it transpired, by a financially stretched doctor and his sister, though how they came to own it, we never did find out. In their absence, a 'caretaker' called June ran it for them along the lines of a very rough nightclub. But as far as I could see, there wasn't a great deal of care being taken of anything. One wing of the house was being used as a makeshift recording studio; the less derelict areas hosted the kind of parties that could easily have ended up with a police raid. The rest of the house was simply being allowed to slip away peacefully in its sleep. We went back one afternoon to find one of these parties in full swing. 'Good Lord,' breathed my mother as we emerged into the courtyard. There was someone asleep in the knot garden wrapped up in a Welsh flag and there were people dressed up as pikemen on the roof tipping beer onto people's heads down below. It seemed we had gatecrashed a Civil War re-enactment party, though Peter remarked that their costumes were more reminiscent of *Star Wars* than any civil war he could think of. It turned out to be the annual gathering of a group of cut-throat fanatics, who had formed their own splinter battalion after being thrown out of the English Civil War Society for being too rough. In the house, huge, toothless women in smocks stoked fires of bonfire proportions and groups of youths, wearing Mad Max jerkins and Doc Martens, honed flick knives on the soft sandstone of a door-surround. My mother edged her way carefully round a body in a sleeping bag, while Peter eyed something on the fire which looked suspiciously like oak panelling.

It was the first time we had met June. We were taken to the Hall of Justice which had a bar in it, with a row of optics behind, screwed straight into the crumbling surface of a Tudor fireplace. June was a small, round, tough-looking woman. She seemed a little sad to me, as though the hardness of her features blanketed some deeper, inner despair. She was a publican by trade. You could tell she'd seen a thing or two in her life: perhaps smacked a few heads together, maybe punched the lights out of a few drunken troublemakers in her time. When she knew our business, she pulled out some glasses and a bottle of gin from behind the bar. Not wishing to appear stand-offish, we accepted her offer of a drink. We made friends very quickly after that. She pushed a bubbling cauldron of sweet-smelling stew towards my mother. It was never emptied, June admitted proudly, just added to for extra flavour.

With the *tush*, *tush*, *tush* of house music in the background June told us that the doctor was on the verge of selling the castle. I felt my heart leap in my chest and thanked the gods of impeccable timing for arranging such a moment in my life. As she scribbled down his telephone number on the back of a beer mat, a football came whizzing through the air and landed behind the bar, knocking over several long-stemmed glasses and a bottle of cherry brandy. I winced inwardly every time I heard its plastic skin thud against the last remaining fragments of Elizabethan plasterwork. 'Jason ger 'ere before I lose my temper,' yelled June. It wasn't the moment for undiplomatic gestures but I felt there were comparisons to be drawn with the story of the moneylenders in the temple. A plastic skull lit up by a fluorescent green light grinned at me from an alcove beneath a sign that said, 'To the Dungeon'.

A dark carnival atmosphere cloaked the whole pro-ceedings. A man in a jester's outfit came in leading a small mud-matted pony. The pony shook itself down and a cloud of dust floated up to the fake beamed ceiling. Two pints of beer were pulled, one for the jester and one for the pony.

The glass was tilted to the pony's lips and when it had finished it slapped a long limb-like tongue around its mouth and rested a pellucid hoof on the floorboards. Its eyelids drooped and it dozed contentedly while the jester regaled us with tales of ghosts and secret passages, which apparently ran from the house to the river. Each time he laughed, mostly at his own jokes, the bell on the end of his hat tinkled. There was even talk of treasure which had been smuggled to America and rumours of a Japanese consortium who wanted to demolish the house and rebuild it on the outskirts of Tokyo. The castle, he told us, had had a very chequered modern history: damaged by fire in 1922, it had been abandoned until 1944, when it was restored by a retired bank manager from Lancashire called Arthur Clegg. It had changed hands at least five times in the last ten years.

We left as some kind of argument was brewing in the Solar Tower between two drunken musketeers and a pikeman. 'You'll have to excuse me now, ducks,' said June, slipping off her bar stool, 'I've got some serious business to attend to in the other room.'

We went out blinking like moles into the bright sunshine, hardly noticing the two fat rats basking in a bed of weeds, or the septic tank which was depositing its semi-raw contents all over the lower lawn. We stopped in Llanrwst on the way home. June and her entourage, we discovered, were known locally as the Addams Family.

There was no doubt about it, Gwydir was a fairly grown-up proposition by anyone's standards. A national heritage body with limitless funds available would have baulked at the prospect of taking it on – what hope was there then for two penniless fantasists without proper jobs? According to the jester, the National Trust had been offered the castle but had turned it down on the grounds that there was no endowment fund available to pay for its restoration. Thinking of Gwydir in terms of commercial viability seemed a kind of sacrilege to me, like eating caviar off a communion wafer. The term 'white elephant' cropped up constantly in relation to the house, but I knew that if I had to choose between a white and a grey elephant, I'd plump for the white one every time.

Once we learnt of Gwydir's existence we threw up London for good. There was no going back. For sale or not, it didn't matter. We would have slept in cardboard boxes outside its gate just to be close to it, just to be sure it didn't go the same way as that old farmhouse, or didn't get taken down stone by stone to be resurrected somewhere on the outskirts of Tokyo. No other house existed for us. We agreed simply to bide our time and wait. And while we waited we rented a house in Flintshire from a friend. It was close enough to Gwydir to keep an eye on it. We were fortunate in that we did not need to be tied to London for work; our livelihoods were portable. The restoration of antiquarian books required surprisingly little space and few tools. Peter, in the meantime, had found himself a freelance job with Cadw, the heritage branch of the Welsh Office, listing houses of architectural merit. It produced interesting responses from the owners. Some people welcomed the scheme but most railed against the interference from the state. It was depressing and rewarding at the same time, and it meant he could work from home. He kept telling himself it was only temporary, once we had Gwydir, he would give it up and become a painter.

'You're going to do what?' squealed Graham, an architect friend, over tea, one eyebrow flickering nervously like the needle on a pressure gauge.

'We're going to buy Gwydir Castle.'

'That's the most lunatic thing I've ever heard. It's the size of a small village, it's Grade I-listed and what's more it's falling down. You'll be ruined if you buy it,' he said, wagging a Ginger Nut at us.

'But what a way to go,' said Peter, with a look reminiscent of Bernini's 'Ecstasy of St Teresa' on his face. Graham appealed to me for sanity. I shrugged my shoulders, complicit in my silence.

'Just you think again before you do anything rash, that's all.' But we had thought again; we could think of nothing else. Images of the house kept floating through our minds like stills from a moody '60s film: the golden light hitting the windowpanes; the desiccated jackdaw, beautiful in death upon the floor of the old nursery; the thought of waking up in the stony embrace of those dark halls. That faraway look on Peter's face said it all. Graham was forced to yield to the united front of blind determination.

'I didn't even know it was for sale,' he said, changing tack slightly.

'Well, it isn't exactly.'

'Darling children, if you're determined to proceed with

this hare-brained scheme then take a tip from your Uncle Graham: first catch your hare.'

He had a point. Perhaps it was time to do something constructive instead of whiling away the hours in a state of tortured, hopeful anxiety. I extracted the crumpled beer mat from my pocket which I'd carried around like a talisman for weeks. 'What's the harm in asking?' I wondered aloud. Peter said that the harm in asking was that the doctor might say no. I took a deep breath and dialled the number. We were about to discover that some hares can run very fast indeed.

The doctor, a psychiatrist by profession, was a shadowy figure. We met him only once. He came to my mother's house – the very spit of Freud, in his tweed suit and pince-nez. His blonde companion seemed silent and tense, though this was due, we later learnt, to the louring presence of Henry, my mother's Great Dane. We offered them tea but the doctor declined. My mother suggested something stronger and a sly smile crept across his bearded face. Collapsing flamboyantly into the soft upholstery of a chintz sofa, he began to tell us of his plans to turn the castle into some kind of conference centre.

'The trouble is,' he concluded, 'my heart just isn't in it any more. I'm getting too old. Perhaps the time has come to pass the torch on to someone else, somebody younger.' He blew his nose, trumpeting loudly into a huge bathsheet of a handkerchief. We sat on the edge of our seats. It had been an agonising decision, he said, but the upkeep was becoming a drain. As far as we could see the 'upkeep' amounted to the installation of the bar and the provision of two urinals in June's flat. But this wasn't the moment to split hairs over semantics.

'And if I sold it to you, what would you do with the castle?'

'Live in it, of course,' said Peter, a touch perplexed by the question. Our plans hadn't proceeded much beyond the point of purchase.

Peering over the edge of his glasses, he gave us the pitying look an asylum nurse might bestow on a particularly bewildered patient. The tips of his fingers danced together, as though he was composing a sonata in his head. My mother, who was in a down-to-earth mood that evening, turned the conversation deftly to money. Her farming roots were never far from the surface, and after five minutes of polite, verbal poker-playing she came straight out with it and said, 'How much for cash?' Peter nearly choked on his drink.

'Ah, I see your mother speaks my kind of language,' the doctor said, winking at me. And they proceeded to hammer it out like two pedlars in a Turkish bazaar. By the end of the evening, we had agreed a figure which was far more than we had, but less than we knew the castle to be worth. It represented the equivalent of a modest terraced house in Clapham, London. I had the sale proceeds from a small cottage my stepfather had left me some years ago and while Peter's income from Cadw was relatively humble, at least it was regular. With a substantial bank loan we could just about raise the asking price, but it left us no money for the restoration or anything to live on. But what did that matter – we'd live on berries from the woods if we had to and the dogs could catch us rabbits. Our overriding fear was that if we didn't buy the castle, some ruthless property speculator would turn the place into a nursing home or would split it into flats – or worse, put chalets on the lower lawn. Given the local authority's track record when it came to preserving historic buildings, we had much to fear.

As they got up to leave, we noticed that the companion's expensive-looking hat had gone missing. The doctor had to guide her out by the arm at this point as my mother's dogs naturally found her reticence towards them fascinating. I retrieved the soggy hat from the jaws of a pug and handed it over. The doctor promised to get in touch the following day, but I knew he wouldn't. I sensed he was the kind of man who never returned telephone calls or answered letters – and I was right. I wondered if he regretted agreeing to such a low asking price, once the effects of the gin had worn off the following morning. In any event, we had plenty of time to ponder all sorts of unlikely scenarios, as the sale, in the end, took eighteen agonising months to complete. But it didn't matter – he'd cast us a thin sliver of hope and it sustained us through those nerve-wracking months. In retrospect, had I been given the option, a jail sentence might have been easier on the nerves. The months passed slowly. In our minds we made consolatory visits to Gwydir and constantly fantasised about what we would do if it ever became ours. In our imaginations, we wandered the overgrown gardens at dusk, restored every room with plasterwork and panelling, and we laid out the formal gardens with fountains and orange trees and even designed a maze for a square of lawn beyond the old yew tree.

Eventually, the doctor contacted us. He was prepared to sell for the price agreed, providing we took it right away with June and her entourage *in situ*. That left us with over half the asking price to raise. And so far, every building society we'd approached had turned us down. Sometimes we got no further than a preliminary telephone enquiry: 'Sorry, madam, we can't process your application because we don't have a tick box for "castle". Also, the age of the building proved to be a problematic sticking point: 'Is it Victorian, Edwardian or modern?' asked the disembodied voice at the other end of the line.

'Tudor,' we said.

'Tudor, is it, I see. And how many rooms might this Tudor castle have?'

'About forty-five, I should think, give or take five either way.'

'Is that so, madam? Next, I expect, you'll be telling me it's haunted.'

We met up with the doctor's bank manager. He was nice and avuncular. We told him our problem. 'I tell you what I'll do,' he said. 'If you take the house complete with June, I'll give you a bank loan for the remaining amount. How about that?'

'Oh yes, please,' we said, nodding like two children who had just thrust their hands into a box of Turkish delight.

'Good. Well that's that, then.' It seemed ungrateful to mention the small matter of interest rates after he'd done us such a good turn. My mother agreed to go guarantor on the loan and the deal was done.

The following day, our solicitor looked deeply troubled when we told him we were buying the castle complete with June and company and that we couldn't see the point of commissioning a structural survey.

'Why ever not?' he said, shaking his head. 'Prudence, after all, is my middle name.' I remember wondering how on earth he'd coped at school with a middle name like that. We explained that we didn't feel obliged to pay for the privilege of being told the place was falling down; we knew that already.

In Sir John Wynn's day, at the close of the sixteenth century, Gwydir stood at the centre of a vast and lucrative estate, its deer park alone occupying some 36,000 acres. When we signed the contract to buy the house, the estate had been reduced in size to just ten acres. Except for the tiny gatehouse in the courtyard and the coach house to the rear, there were no stables or outbuildings to speak of.

The first significant sale of land had taken place in 1896 when whole villages were sold and farms dispersed like ashes on the wind. By some incredibly complicated bit of marital genealogy (which I haven't fully got to the bottom of yet), the house and remaining lands ended up belonging to the Earl of Carrington. In 1921 he sold up and the house passed out of inherited ownership for the first time in over four hundred years. The chapel and summer house, which sit picturesquely up on the hill overlooking the castle, with views down the long, fertile valley almost to the sea, were split off from the house: the chapel was taken into the care of the state and the summer house sold to the Forestry Commission, whose successors still use it today as their regional headquarters. Every field around the house was sold. The fishing on the River Conwy was sold, even the walled garden up by the summer house was sold and two semi-detached houses were built in its confines for the views. Where once there had been cabbages and espaliered pear trees, now there were bonsai and a rockery.

When the searches came back from our solicitor, we discovered that planning permission had indeed been sought by a previous owner to build chalets on the lower lawn. Mercifully, for whatever reason, the house had been spared that final indignity.

3
Moving In

I now only have to smell Jeyes Fluid and I am back there clearing up the squalor after June left. It was 1st November. Peter had chosen the date for moving in with care, as 350 years ago to the day the house had been sacked during the Civil War. It felt a portentous anniversary.

There was no ceremonial handing over of the keys, as there were no keys to hand over. Those doors that could be locked, were locked from behind by huge rusting bolts which rasped into place – the rest were just left open, or at best propped from behind with timber supports. Miraculously, two days earlier, the squatters had responded to reasoned dialogue and had agreed to go peacefully. We arrived as they were in the throes of leaving. June had already departed. It felt like a circus packing up and leaving town. Indignant geese were being shoved into hessian sacks, caravans were hooked on to the back of pickup trucks, beer pullers were detached and drum kits dismantled. Only one or two uncatchable cockerels remained by the end of the day, scared up onto the gatehouse roof. Horns were sounded and the roar of revving engines echoed down the valley. With a huge sense of relief we closed the car park gates behind them. We'd arrived with our two dogs, Carw and Madoc, and as many useless provisions as you could fit into one car.

It was getting dark. We hadn't seen Gwydir at night before. Peter and I walked back along the path beneath the shelves of the cedar branches with the dogs trotting proudly ahead, and though everything was new and rather dream-like to me, I felt calm and settled as though the worst leg of a long journey was over. It was as though our lives had been split in two by the downward stroke of a giant scimitar: this moment represented a crossroads at which point our lives were changed for ever.

The sight of the house lit up by candles made us stop as we came into the courtyard. Candlelight is the best light to see anything by. It hid all the undesirable reminders of the work we had in front of us and just showed us the best of the house. The towering chimneys were silhouetted against the sky and the candlelight glinted against the leaded panes, deepening the orange glow and illuminating the beams in the Hall of Meredith. The night was so still our voices echoed around the courtyard, ricocheting against the castle walls and the vast bulk of the hill on our left. We could hear the peacocks settling for the night high up in the branches of the cedars. The house took on a different personality altogether in the dark. It was more secretive, less expansive and very mysterious. Peter put an arm around my shoulders and led me into the house. There was no electricity in the ground-floor halls. But not even candlelight could disguise the mess in these rooms: the smell alone reminded me of the Herculean task that lay ahead of us. I decided there was no point starting anything at that time of night, so I took myself off to explore bedroom options. Climbing the spiral staircase with your hands full required a good deal of concentration. It was amazing to think that all those feet over the years had actually worn down the steps. You had to let your feet fall naturally into the dips in the stone without thinking about it and then let the rest of your body follow suit. The trouble came when you tried to be diligent about placing your feet in the hollows. Too much care ruined the flow and the result was an inelegant scramble on all fours. The hot wax from the candle I carried trickled down the back of my hand, which I ended up feeling quite grateful for as the temperature was less than hospitable inside the house.

The Hall of Meredith was an impossible place to hurry through. It just asked to be admired. I put on a few more jumpers and sat on the window seat with my back against a stone mullion. The windowpanes didn't rattle as they do in Victorian novels, they just tinkled, but it was a comforting sound. The candle cast marvellous shadows up to the arch-braced collar trusses of the roof. This part of the house was remodelled around 1500 and was named after Meredith ap Ieuan ap Robert, the founder of the Wynn dynasty, though the hall itself was thought to have been built two generations earlier by Howel Coetmore, a dashing commander of longbowmen who had served in the Hundred Years War. But it was Meredith ap Ieuan I'd developed rather a soft spot for. He was both brave and vulnerable and never went anywhere without his hand-picked bodyguard of twenty tall bowmen, so afraid was he of being assassinated. During his lifetime it was recorded that he fathered over twenty children, with three wives and four concubines. The hall I now sat in spoke most strongly of him.

Somewhere outside, in the darkness of the trees, a screech owl called to its mate. Apart from that there was real silence. I had never known such a quiet house. From where I sat I could see stars filling the heavens and a shaft of moonlight came in through a window which fell in a triangle across the floorboards. Because of its position on the valley floor, the castle sits quite snugly in a bowl of hills. The lights of the little farmhouses on the opposite slopes twinkled intermittently and in the foreground I could see the black outline of the cypress trees edging the garden.

As I sat there in the blue light, picking the dried candle wax from the back of my hand, I began to think about all the other past inhabitants of the house, which in turn gave me a tremendous sense of my own mortality, though not in a depressing way. I thought of the poor serving maid who supposedly haunted the house and wondered if the story was true or not. This serving maid was apparently on intimate terms with Sir John Wynn who, having seduced her and made her pregnant, then, for some unexplained reason, decided to murder her and wall her up within a large void in one of the chimney breasts, about five feet away from where I was sitting. It was the smell of her decomposing body which exposed his ghastly crime and he allegedly made a deathbed confession admitting to the murder. A scurry of small feet in the rafters made me jump; a door slammed in some far-off part of the castle.

I gathered up my papers, picked up my candle stub and made my way down a lop-sided corridor in search of Peter. This corridor connected the hall range to the Solar Tower and about halfway down I passed a medieval garderobe, or toilet, on my right. A medieval garderobe, apparently, not only served as a toilet, but also doubled as a wardrobe where you hung your fur-lined robes so that the ammonia fumes rising up from the drain shaft would kill the lice and fleas in your clothes. I hoped I would not have to resort to the same technique. I lifted my candle and peered down into the deep shaft: there was moss growing on the inner walls and the sound of dripping water far below. At the very bottom was an opening which disappeared horizontally into darkness, wide enough for a man to crawl along on all fours. This was the secret passage the jester had spoken about – not a secret passage at all, but the garderobe drain which ran through the house, originally taking the effluent off to the River Conwy. Locally, Gwydir was a hotbed of popular myth and it was going to take a good deal of effort and persuasion to shake off the dungeons and dragons image it had acquired in recent years.

I could hear knocking coming from the Solar Tower. I followed the sound. The doves were roosting in the Great Chamber, fluffing their feathers and purring. I crept down the second spiral staircase which gave access to all the floors in the Solar Tower and on the ground floor I found Peter halfway up a vast chimney on a ladder. He came down sheepishly when I called, covered in soot and with a tear in the knee of his trousers.

'Just looking for priestholes,' he said, as though it was the most ordinary thing in the world. He was exploring a theory that Sir John Wynn's overt Protestantism may have been a smokescreen for deeper, recusant sympathies. My concerns were more prosaically centred on where we were to spend the night. Our options were fairly limited: the choice ranged between the floor of the Hall of Meredith or the floor of a tiny boxroom in the wing that June had just vacated. I was all for braving one of the great halls, preferring romantic squalor to fake squalor, but I lost my nerve after deciding that the rats – and the house was seething with them – would probably love the amenity of burrowing into sleeping bags. The doves, too, were a disincentive to a good night's sleep, as was the thought of bats, particularly when Peter pointed out that unlike most animals, bats are deficient in the sphincter muscle department, which effectively makes them airborne toilets.

We hadn't thought to bring essentials such as firelighters and torches. What we had classed as essentials were candlesticks, books and pewter plates, but none of these were of much use to us now. We found an old damp mattress which June had left behind and covered it with the bubble wrap which our pewter had been packaged in. It was too cold to undress. We lay down in our clothes and tried to persuade ourselves that it was very comfortable indeed. Carw, being the furrier of our two dogs, was more warming than Peter so I snuggled up to her. Moonlight came in and made devilish faces in the bubbling pink plaster. There were interesting specimens of mould all over the house, but the most spectacular were in the boxroom. It was a whitish fungus, as soft as an earlobe, with a brown edge, which crept down the corner of the walls where the rainwater had seeped in over the years from beneath the cracked leads. It was dry rot. I've become an expert in household fungi since those days and can tell wet rot from dry rot at a hundred paces, blindfold.

We couldn't sleep for excitement, so Peter read me

extracts from a Civil War commentary on the Royalist troops arriving at Gwydir on the night of 1 November 1645. It was recorded that after the disastrous Battle of Denbigh Green, the Royalist commander, 'fled with the remainder of his horse, in number nine hundred, towards the mountains and fell that night upon the house of Sir Richard Wynn, where they stayed five days, and, on going, rifled the house'. The fact that it was a Royalist house hadn't spared it from a hoodlum sacking.

We listened out for the sound of horses' hooves on cobblestones, but except for the groans and the creaks of an old house settling in its sleep there was silence. A wind got up in the middle of the night and made the house moan gently: a soft whistling in the chimney stack; the flapping of a loose tarpaulin somewhere on the roof. And then every so often, the more localised sound of popping bubble wrap as Peter turned in his sleep, which once or twice during the night I mistook for musket fire. A door slammed somewhere below us and the Expelair in the downstairs Gents whirred like an angry animal. I slept in snatches and woke feeling tired and chilled to the bone. But at least it was light and I could cross the house safely without fear of falling through a hole in the floor.

4
Trial by Pestilence and Flood

*Y*esterday, between the showers, the sun came out and it felt like being given a big bar of chocolate after a six-week fast. Spring is very late this year and the weather refuses to warm up. I felt the sun was trying to trick the buds into coming out, but they won't be fooled; all the trees are holding out for weather that doesn't have frost up its sleeve. The peacocks seem to realise it's spring before anything else does, though I rather wish they wouldn't, as the noise is suddenly deafening after their long winter silence. They have been here since 1828, though someone told me recently that they left briefly after the fire in 1922, but came back again when they discovered that someone was prepared to feed them corn. It is very difficult to keep them out of the house, as they have long been used to having the run of the place and it is not uncommon to find a peacock perched on a coffer pecking at candle wax which, for some reason, they appear to consider a delicacy.

Gwydir has its own separate microclimate from the rest of the valley. There can be a heatwave outside and still it will be freezing inside. I have noticed that it takes weeks for the house to adjust to a change in the weather and then only by a few degrees either way. I don't think the temperature inside has ever got into double figures on the thermometer. Even now, after all the effort we have put into restoring the house, the walls are still damp and are very efficient at not letting the warm air penetrate. Will Pierce, our stonemason from Betws-y-Coed, tells us that wet walls dry out at a rate of one inch per year. Our walls are ten feet thick in places, thus complex mathematics are required to work out how long it will be before we can go without coats inside during the winter months.

The kind of rain we've been having lately reminds me of the weather we suffered during the first week of moving in. The Welsh say '*Mae'n bwrw hen wragedd a ffyn*' – 'it's raining old women and sticks' – and I can quite see what they're getting at, as Welsh rain is the most pernicious rain of all, particularly the kind that sweeps horizontally off the mountains and has the capacity to find a weak spot in any waterproof garment. It was the kind of rain that slid under doorways and coursed down chimneys. It drenched the peacocks and turned their beautiful blue necks to an opalescent green. The house felt like a boat come loose from its moorings and if that first week was a voyage of discovery, then it left us feeling moderately shipwrecked by the end.

The first day started well enough. The excitement of actually waking at Gwydir cast a rose-tinted glow upon every mildewed surface. We feasted heartily on a breakfast of crisps and satsumas and warmed ourselves up with tea brewed on a Primus stove. And then there was nothing for it but to plunge into the spread of toil that awaited us. We scrubbed a great many of the rooms within an inch of their lives and it felt marvellously liberating to be doing something positive after all the months of frustrating inactivity. The house suddenly seemed to come alive, as though it was thanking us for getting rid of the modern eyesores, such as the bar and its 'ye olde' fake ceiling beams. The music we played had a great cleansing effect, too. Peter said he thought the house would rebel if it had to listen to anything later than 1690, so we played mostly early music: Guillaume Dufay and Abbess Hildegard of Bingen, which lifted the spirit of the place magnificently. Our priority for the first week was to try to make at least two rooms fit for human habitation. A good deal of rubbish had been left behind in the house: not old, antiquey rubbish among which everyone dreams of finding an old master, but modern, ugly rubbish, of the kind that takes an inordinate amount of effort to get rid of. We sang sea shanties as we hauled the beer-stained carpets down to a bonfire in the car park. Sven brought up the rear with a squeaking wheelbarrow full of net curtains and broken bits of Formica. I hadn't the talent to make things burn without firelighters then; now I've had so much practice I could probably make water burn. Getting the sodden pile to ignite would have challenged the most ardent pyromaniac, but not Sven – a can of paraffin skilfully aimed at the centre of the pyre and in minutes we had a blaze of which to be proud.

Earlier on in the day, while exploring one of the cellars, or 'dungeons' as June had called them, Peter found a plastic skeleton chained to a wall. We liberated it with a hacksaw and gave it a piggyback down to the bonfire where it made an excellent, if rather eerie guy, perched on top of the blaze with the flames licking through its ribcage. The skeleton is frequently enquired after now and I am forced to recount its sad fate to a reception of horrified stares. In June's day, visitors to the castle were apparently told that the skeleton was a real prisoner left to starve in chains in the dungeon, after being caught poaching on the estate by Sir John

Wynn. The jester dined out on the story of how his moans could be heard echoing through the house on quiet, moonless nights.

There was a tremendous feeling of camaraderie among us workers. My mother had pitched up looking like an ageing Land Army girl in dungarees and a rather fetching plaid turban. Jerry, a friend from the south, had also offered his assistance in return for bed and board. Bed meant a lilo on a cold flagstone floor and board meant anything which could be heated up quickly on a Primus stove, and washed down with as much cheap claret as you could drink. He was a jovial, ex-military type often given to boisterous bursts of unnecessary bonhomie. He was more a friend of my mother's than he was of ours and we couldn't now remember how the arrangement had come about. I saw Peter raise a wary eyebrow at the immaculate vertical creases in his trousers.

Another friend who had access to a van at weekends had kindly delivered our furniture for us. It sat in a pile in the courtyard waiting to find lodgings inside. It was furniture of the most impractical kind: very heavy and too precious to use. Our ancient chairs were held together by a honeycomb of woodworm holes. Nothing we possessed could be pressed into useful service. Around the huge inglenook fireplace in the Lower Hall were gathered an eclectic assortment of upturned buckets.

We struggled with the fire. It was our only source of heat in the house. A year's worth of combustibles sat piled up in the grate. Peter poked around and extracted two forlorn bits of charred seventeenth-century panelling. Otherwise, the mound mainly consisted of takeaway trays and plastic milk cartons. We constructed a wigwam of knotted newspaper and damp twigs over the top of the mound and set it alight. Instantly, a cloud of noxious fumes billowed out into the room. Fires are notoriously difficult to put out once ignited and there was nothing for it but to press on regardless with the bellows. It was hell on the eyes and I cursed the ingenuity of the jackdaws. Soon a small flame took hold and the fire burst into life. The flames must have dislodged something in the chimney as a shower of valuable dry kindling rained down. I praised the generosity of the jackdaws. Just as the fog was beginning to clear in the room, a small bomb surprised us by exploding in the fireplace and a smoking missile sailed out of the grate and hit Peter on the leg.

'I'm hit,' he cried. I looked down and saw a viscous yellow substance oozing out between his fingers. The most awful smell ensued. I couldn't make sense of it at first. Why did Peter have yellow blood suddenly? Had he contracted some strange, alien disease? And then a second missile burst out of the flames and landed at my feet on the flagstones – a quivering pool of opaque jelly with a yellow heart – an egg! Some enterprising chicken had evidently hopped into the fireplace a long time ago and had laid a clutch of eggs deep in the warm heart of the paper mound.

We sat around the fire in the Lower Hall that night. Jerry had produced a celebratory dinner of mussels and oysters from the little harbour in Conwy. The Primus stove hissed contentedly away on the flagstones, producing its own unique aroma of onions, gas and seashells. Everyone but Sven had boycotted the kitchen after finding rat droppings in the cupboards and the bloated body of a dead rat in the water tank which supplied the kitchen. We'd made an effort with the furnishings having brought in a few pieces from the courtyard. It was good for morale. Our new home might be a derelict shell but at least now it was, in part, an elegantly furnished derelict shell. We spread a Turkish carpet across the flagstones and dressed a little gateleg table with candlesticks and pewter. Our furniture, as impractical as it was, fitted perfectly into its new surroundings: it was as though it had been waiting for a castle to live in all its life, so that it could show off the best of itself. I retrieved a bottle of champagne from the leg of a wellington boot which I'd been saving for such an occasion, and we sat and ate a blissful meal of oysters and *moules marnière* with thick slices of granary bread from the bakery in Llanrwst, spread thickly with creamy Welsh butter.

My limbs ached with fatigue but I had never felt so elated, so happy. We raised our glasses in the candlelight and watched the fire illuminate the dark, sooty recesses of the inglenook. We opened the door; it was warmer out than in. The night air brought in sweet draughts of rain-rinsed vegetation and earth. I sat basking in the winter perfume of the garden, noticing every moment some new aspect of the hall we sat in. The few poor fragments of remaining plasterwork above the fireplace were just visible beneath a canopy of cobwebs: two fleurs-de-lis, a lion baring its teeth, and an ostrich with impossibly long legs. Even now, five years on, the sense of wonder I felt that night has never left me. I felt humbled by the weight of all that history bearing down upon me and the knowledge that it was up to us now to breathe life back into it again. I couldn't help wondering by what magic we'd ended up here. As insignificant as I thought myself to be I felt there was a reason, and the knowledge that Divine Providence might have had a hand in orchestrating our fate filled me with an energy I had not known before.

Four minutes after this edifying thought had entered my head, I was on my knees throwing up in the pink bathroom. Instinctively, I knew it had something to do with the oysters.

I suspect there are moments in everyone's life when the glamour of a long-awaited happening wears off and one is left staring into the face of cold, implacable reality. One such moment occurred in my life the next morning, when I awoke from a night spent dealing with the effects of acute seafood poisoning without the provision of an upstairs flushable loo. It was a degrading business made worse by the knowledge that there was no hot water to be had either. All night I writhed on my mattress of bubble wrap, listening to the metallic plink of rainwater hitting a rusted Fray Bentos tin in the corner of June's old bedroom. The weather was wild, wickedly wild and wet. A blistering sea wind chased the rain up the valley from the north and it drummed its briny fingers against the windows. I prayed our teetering chimney stacks would stand firm and not be coaxed to suicide by the wind. Though poleaxed by waves of nausea, part of me still fretted about the remaining furniture exposed to the elements in the courtyard; but when I tried to alert someone, I realised my throat had constricted (from continuous retching) to the diameter of a piece of macaroni, and when I tried to lift myself off the floor my legs refused to engage with the rest of my body. I vaguely acknowledged the possibility that I might be hallucinating when I saw the white fungus in the corner of the room spewing out of the cracks in the walls like shaving foam and advancing across the floor towards my makeshift bed. I also thought I could hear a roar of water beneath my bedroom window, of a kind that usually denotes a hidden closeness to the sea. I imagined I could hear waves lapping at the house and the bleat of sheep, which became intermingled with the mew of seagulls and the tearing of tarpaulins as the wind whipped about inside the house. My one moment of lucid thought came in a flash when I fathomed the meaning of the DWR and EMER graffiti. The leak in the bedroom ceiling emanated from a chalked DWR and landed on an EMER, which had been sprayed onto the bare boards, now happily covered by the Fray Bentos tin. *Dwr*, I suddenly remembered, was the Welsh word for water and *emer*, the word for bucket.

I finally dozed and when I awoke I felt recovered enough to picture myself in a sickbed scene where the nurse looks up and with her hand on my brow says, 'God have mercy, the fever's left her, ma'am.' Peter, I noticed, was nowhere to be seen. I thought I could hear faint murmuring coming from the room next door. The dogs were lying across my sleeping bag, pinning me in like tent pegs. I struggled out and still on my knees I made it down the corridor where I found him on his back surrounded by dunes of Kleenex tissues and the miserable jetsam of the sickbay. We both tried to speak but except for the odd monosyllable, there was not a sensible conversation to be had from either of us.

The next thing I knew, Jerry came bounding into the room and told us in one, long, sausaged-out sentence that the river had burst its banks in the night and the garden was completely flooded and that we were cut off from the town and all our garden walls had been washed away and the cellars were full of water and the flood was still rising and some of our furniture was still outside in the courtyard and our car was floating around in the car park. And what did we want him to do? That was the moment reality hit. Not even I could kid myself that there was romance to be found in our current predicament. A jackdaw cawed mockingly down the chimney. I suffered an overwhelming pang of self-pity and buried my head in a damp, sick-scented pillow.

There is a causeway at the bottom of our garden. It crosses our neighbour's marshy field and stops at the river. There are steps leading up to it and steps leading down from it. The idea was that you could walk along the top of it to the river without getting your feet wet and then climb into your barge and sail down to Conwy. Sir John Wynn had it built sometime during the 1580s and later it became known as the Chinese Walk, though no one is certain why. Its presence perhaps should have alerted us to the prospect of river-flooding. No one had mentioned the fact that our garden was technically still part of the flood plain and was thus susceptible to regular dousings from the River Conwy. Instead, we were left to discover for ourselves what it was to wake up aboard the Ark. Even the doves, it occurred to me, were playing their part, flying in and out of the Great Chamber on scouting missions to find dry land.

Thankful at last that the oysters had piped down, I found my sea legs and went to the window. The sight that greeted me was almost too surreal to comprehend. The garden on the north side of the house, or the Dutch Garden as it is called, had been completely flooded by the river. It was as though Capability Brown had been employed to work his magic with an ornamental lake. There was no grass to be seen, only the spectral vision of the avenue of yew trees sitting up to their waists in peat-brown water. It looked like a prehistoric swamp shrouded in bog mists, with the ragged stones of quartz and dead flag iris poking out from around the fountain basin. The wall at the bottom of the garden had indeed been strewn across the B5106. Water was now streaming through the gaping wounds, spilling out boulders as though they were pebbles. A single, lone gatepier stood defiant; its partner had put up a valiant struggle but the pressure of water had proved too much.

Sometime later, the weekly newspaper reported statistics that propelled our flood into the annals of local legend. The Environment Agency claimed that the Conwy Valley had experienced a-one-in-a-hundred-year flood and that the water was leaving the grounds of Gwydir Castle at the rate of a hundred thousand gallons per second. It was a comfort to learn our flood was an aberration of nature and not a normal run-of-the-mill flood. Perhaps this was as bad as it would ever get. If we just held on tight it would soon go away and we could resume the task of getting to know our garden. I wondered how the moles were faring down there in sea world.

Apparently, we suffered the worst of the flooding in our corner of the valley because the local farmer who owned the causeway fields had refused to pay his cob tax way back in the '50s, and the cob walls, which had once kept the water confined to the riverbed, had been allowed to break down. The implications of regular floods were lost on me then. Perhaps out of a sense of sheer self-preservation, I failed to comprehend what it would take to restore a Grade I-listed garden, given that it spent half its life under water. As I stood in the Hall of Meredith watching the ducks slaloming in and out of the yew trees, I was thankful that, except for the cellars, the flood waters hadn't reached the house.

'It could have been worse,' I heard myself whispering against the thin, aqueous glass of an ancient windowpane. This harmless little phrase was to become a kind of mantra over the coming weeks. We felt like the victims of some bizarre initiation rite, in which plague, pestilence and flood had all played their part.

It was no hallucination; I had heard sheep bleating outside the window. Sven had waded into the rising flood and rescued several sodden ewes out of the icy waters and they stood steaming and dazed beneath the sheltering walls of the house. I watched the dawn breaking over the far hill beyond the garden trees. The light glinted on the surface of the water. It was calmer now, as though the storm had left suddenly in a fit of pique and only the breeze from its coat tails remained to pucker the water. Abstract bands of colour swiped the sky: the pure white of the horizon, dazzling against the blackness of the hill; a wash of featherbed pink; and then the palest strip of blue which fused imperceptibly with the distant dark of the faraway heavens. From the Hall of Meredith I could see the two stone arms of the castle's flanking wings stretching out into the garden. The tarpaulins had vanished from the roof of the west wing to reveal the skeleton structure of rafters and purlins inside, like the bones of a desert carcass. Peter joined me and together we peered out of the window. If there was ever a moment of doubt, this was it. For the first time I became aware of the sacrifices we would have to make to restore this house. I wondered if our youth and relative lack of experience would go against us. I thought of the comforts of the rented house we'd left behind: electric lights at the flick of a switch, hot water at the turn of a tap. It was like the phantom image of a cool glass of water to one who is parched. As if in answer to my question, Peter said: 'You know we can do it. We'll take our time, but in the end we'll get there.' In all this, the only thing I was certain of was Peter. As long as we had each other I knew we could see this through.

We stared for a long time out of the window. We were soon whisked away by the beauty of it all again. It was such an unusual-looking house. Sometimes it seemed to me as though it had been conjured out of the damp earth by sorcery. The fact that it had taken over five hundred years to mature gave it such dignity. The patina was just right, the slate stone was the perfect mixture of lichened grey and ochre, and the oak gates leading into the courtyard had weathered to a silvery hue, the colour of a grey mare's tail. Peter squeezed my hand and all doubt vanished in the wink of a peacock's eye.

The following morning, there was nothing for it but to hurl ourselves into the day in an effort to leapfrog the torpid state of convalescence for which our bodies craved. I slithered uneasily down the spiral staircase, gripping the stone newel post like an inexperienced fireman. Jerry was frying up a hearty breakfast of bacon and eggs on the Primus stove. The smell of the fry-up almost masked the own-brand body odour of the house, but not quite. June's two dogs had once savaged a sheep and from that day on they had spent their lives imprisoned inside the castle, free-roaming and liberal with their excretions. Urinary precedents had been created at every corner and Madoc, the younger of our two dogs, was determined to cover every scent with his own. And who could blame him: inside was more like outside here; there were dark, irresistibly earthy corners in almost every room. The accumulated smell of dog and stale beer, the sweat from disco bodies, cigarettes, municipal disinfectant, damp ash and fungus overlaid by bacon and eggs seared itself to the inside of my nostrils. I swallowed hard.

Jerry roared a greeting. 'No point moping about in bed,'eh!' He slapped my back, hard. I just managed to grasp the edge of the table in time to prevent myself collapsing in a heap on the flagstones. At least he'd got the fire going.

'That's the last of the wood,' he boomed.

I bolted for the door, unable to stomach the spectacle of a slab of fried bread wading into a lagoon of tomato sauce and rheumy egg. A gentle perambulation through the house was all I felt I could manage. Though we'd lived in the house for just under a week, I still kept losing my bearings and constantly had to remind myself where the kitchen was in relation to our bedroom and how the maze of other rooms interrelated.

The house rather conveniently separated itself into four (un)manageable blocks: the Solar Tower, the hall range,; the east wing and the west wing. I went off to explore the west wing first. I had visited it only twice before. This was the wing that Lord Willoughby d'Eresby had built for his invalid daughter, Elizabeth. It was a faithful copy of the older, flanking wing – the two arms reaching out into the Dutch Garden and between them, in the U, a sheltered bit of garden with overgrown borders that hugged the walls of the house. The architect, Sir Charles Barry, had built the wing from scratch in 1828. So good was it, in fact, that it had fooled many an amateur historian into thinking it was ancient.

This wing contained yet more empty, cavernous rooms. On the first floor: the King's Room, the Duke of Beaufort's Chamber and a bathroom full of modern jumble, its walls crudely constructed out of bits of old panelling. The undergrowth which crowded in through the window made the room so dark you couldn't quite see what you were touching – was that a leather glove, a leaf or a withered hand down there in the corner? There was a rusty bicycle poking out of an enormous enamel bath and piles of yellowing newspapers and old plant pots, still full of earth, stacked against the walls. The spiders were impressive. Not thin elegant spiders, which glided effortlessly over difficult surfaces, but spiders with thick black bodies and meaty legs, which only moved when you prodded them, like reluctant old men.

Next, the King's Room. Three chunky oak steps led up into it. It was another huge, church-hall-like space, open to the gaping roof – the desert carcass I'd seen the day before from the opposite wing. It was a sadness to see all the plaster had been hacked from the walls. There were circular saw marks on the wide oak floorboards, reused perhaps from some other part of the house. A winceable parody of a fireplace in pseudo-medieval style had been built into the end wall. The wood-surround which formed the mantelpiece had been constructed out of the post and panel screen from the Lower Hall – the original late fifteenth-century passage screen, no less, which had survived the Civil War and two fires but had not survived an overenthusiastic restoration of the 1940s. Even the door had been fitted with a chunky, mock baronial handle of the kind that Hollywood, *circa* 1930, might have hired as a prop. The room swashed and it most definitely buckled.

The rough, cave-like interior was a far cry from invalid daughters and polite Regency society, or indeed from polite sixteenth- or seventeenth-century society. I could almost hear the old baronet whispering, 'Where has my limehair plaster gone, my wall paintings, my panelling, my sumptuous hangings in silver and gold brocade?' On the face of it the entire house had been stripped down to its underwear and essentially, bar a few spectacular but miraculous survivors, we were left, in some parts, with only walls and windows. The relative lack of fixtures and fittings didn't demean the house for us; on the contrary, that was why we were here. There was a kind of ghostly nostalgia to it all, echoes of what the great house had once been and could be again. We would attempt to blow the dust off its ravaged face and play the alchemist's hand, transmuting a low and unloved drinking den into a wonder, a lovely glowing ruby in Wales's mossy crown. We would stitch up the wound that neglect had made in its past. We would seal up the roofs with love. And those who had written off the dear old house (and there were many), the 'old-buildings-stand-in-the-way-of-progress' types, would one day eat their words.

Such thoughts tripped through my mind as I made my way unsteadily around the house. I wandered down a backstair to a room anachronistically called the Jacobean Room – it was no more Jacobean than I; we were still in Barry's later wing. The ravers had turned it into their recording studio in recent times. The ceiling was lined with polystyrene and the walls hung with sinister black drapes. A trapdoor in the floor led down some stone steps to one of two cellars in the house. I forced myself to lift up the door – I was determined that there would be nothing in this house I would ever be afraid of. A freezing blast of damp air whooshed up through the crack. I inched it open, expecting, what? A flap of wings or two bright glowering eyes staring back at me? Time froze as I peered into the abyss but there was nothing, no sign of life or death, just a sheet of blackness and the drip of water far below. My reserves of courage had been exhausted by this action. I dropped the door back into its snug cradle and moved on.

In the kitchen Peter was industriously occupied making a series of bait stations that, he said, would annihilate the rats. It was a prototype of his own devising and consisted of a thin piece of plastic drainpipe filled liberally with warfarin, which was then secreted in every dark corner of the house. He looked up from his work like some mad Dr Crippen character; a curl of thick dark hair bouncing forward into his excited eyes. He had a suspicion that he had died of the plague in a past life and was determined not to be caught out a second time. A sign had appeared in Peter's hand, taken from the rust-pocked fridge June had left behind, which said, 'Don't take the mickey, Mickey,' beneath which was a drawing of Mickey Mouse in a hangman's noose. The kitchen was a filthy place, full of broken, limping things: half a Formica cupboard abandoned in the corner; a chair with a broken back; several old saucepans without handles; a teapot without a spout. A thick rim of dirt and grease covered every surface. It had an institutionalised feel to it – lots of stainless steel cabinets and broken fire extinguishers, as though a half-hearted attempt had been made to comply with health and safety standards in about 1968; and there were rat runs everywhere behind the cupboards, which appeared to have been imaginatively insulated with all manner of shredded upholstery.

Also, an exotic breed of frog had taken up residence in the corridor outside the kitchen. They were tiny, mottled creatures and I could find no mention of them in Peter's *AA Book of the Countryside*. But frogs I could live with; they were happy souls. I also felt there was a delicate ecosystem at work: the frogs kept the slugs and the silverfish down; the silverfish kept the dust mites down, and so forth. It was the newts that gave me trouble. They inhabited a dingy rear passageway at the back of the house that was now full of water because of the rising flood-level. I was suspicious of their generally furtive behaviour, the way they darted between the flagstones at the sound of an approaching shoe. Somehow, bar the rats, we would all just have to find a way to rub along together.

As I was helping Peter pack the bait stations with warfarin, Jerry came in. I could tell by the cheerful look on his face that there was bad news to come.

'I've got some introductions to make,' he said brightly, and a large blonde lady homed into view behind him.

'We live in your coach house. How do?' she said, wiping her hand on the plateau of her enormous bosom before offering it to me.

'Quite well, thank you,' I lied, which bought me some time while I tried to digest this bombshell piece of information. So this person lived in our coach house and we knew nothing about her! The coach house was not easily visible from the house, hidden as it was behind a large laurel tree, and we'd not yet had time to explore. No one had said anything about a family living in it. Peter and I exchanged horrified glances. She reached behind her and plucked out a small blond child.

'We've just moved Little Jim to the local village school and he's settling down lovely, aren't you, Cat Weasel?' The boy nodded and then proceeded to wipe his chocolate-covered mouth across the tensile sheen of his mother's Lycra pants.

'And this is Lisa.' A sulky, gum-chewing teenage girl emerged, Russian doll-like from behind her mother.

'And this is Lisa's friend, Lynne. And this is my hubby, Big Jim.' The most diminutive man I'd ever seen in my life was dragged out from behind the others and set down before us. He was straight out of Dickens, a clerk or some starveling orphan with a pinched face and yellow hair which crossed from left to right over the top of his head.

'Well, I never did,' Jerry was saying, shaking his head. 'What d'you know?'

A stream of non-stop chatter issued from the woman at breakneck speed. 'And my hubby, he's good with electrics, used to work on the fairgrounds in Porthcawl, and he's willing to work in lieu of rent, and my rice pudding's not half bad so they tell me, but you know what it's like, things get rusty after a time and...' I saw Peter's hands mechanically scooping the poison into the drainpipes as though his ears deceived him.

'...We've got a perfectly good house to go to in Blaenau Ffestiniog, haven't we, Jim? But we love it here, we love it at the castle don't we 'Lisa?' The daughter popped a chewing-gum bubble. 'Well, I could stand here and chat all day, but you know how it is, I've got potatoes to peel and chickens to feed. And just you remember, anything we can do to help and we'll be right over – we're neighbours now, see?'

No, I didn't see. I didn't see at all and neither did Peter by the look on his face. A great ocean of laughter boomed around the walls and then she turned and her silent family followed her, crocodile fashion, out of the room.

When the flood waters receded from the garden a few days later, we were left with a four-metre-wide tidemark of detritus to clear up, which consisted mostly of larch needles, old plimsolls, Coke cans and drowned hedgehogs. And a strange phenomenon occurred that has not been witnessed before or since. Every earthworm in the garden appeared to have risen to the surface and drowned. A walk around the garden was a ghastly trudge through a sludge of bodies until a flock of seagulls moved in like a white mist and gathered them all up, reminding me that though we lived among mountains, the sea was but a few bowshots away.

A copy of *Hard Times* had also been washed up on the flood. Apt, under the circumstances, I thought. I went round with my trug gathering the strewn pages off the heads of last season's thistles, as though the garden had yielded a crop of words for me to harvest.

5
Restoration Dramas

'Let's look on the bright side,' said Peter, another mantra hatching on his lips. 'We could do with an electrician.'

We sat before the fire sipping warmed-up claret from chipped enamel mugs. It was impossible to get an even toasting from any of these fires. One side of my face was crisping up nicely. The other side was iceberg cold from the chill of the enormous room that unfurled like a flag behind me. Wellington boots were the only footwear that accommodated three pairs of thick socks comfortably. I could smell the rubber of the soles softening up, yielding to the warm embers of the fire.

It was silly of us not to have inspected the coach house the minute we took up residence, but there was so much else to attend to – so much else to occupy every waking hour of that first week. The minute the Busbys' car had left the car park, we had sped over to the coach house to take a look. It was an odd little building. It sat bang up against the road, and the road of course had risen over the years. Its origins were certainly old. There was a two-storey tower with little arrow slits for windows. Peter thought it may once have been a dovecote, which no doubt kept the castle well stocked with pigeon pie and other winged delicacies during the lean winter months. In the nineteenth century, an extension was added and it became the coach house, with room enough for just one coach. In the 1950s it was brutally converted to a house. It now resembled a forlorn mongrel of a building – a disfigured victim of bad architectural surgery. But in spite of this, it still had charm.

A big old laurel tree smothered out the sun and the wooded hill behind kept the walls humidified with damp and forest spores. I rubbed at a mildewed pane with the sleeve of my jumper and we both peered in. I had last seen such an interior in Cairo where a family of eight and two donkeys all lived together in one room. The social services would have condemned it instantly had they seen it. I pushed the door open a crack and a rippling bank of heat almost bowled me over. A two-bar electric fire was churning out that stifling, roasted dust aroma, and the squalor of overcrowded habitation (compounded by a leaking roof) was not a sight to cockle-warm the heart. The air was as stale as a coffin's. Still, to use estate agent's parlance, the coach house had 'potential' for those with eyes to see. There really was 'a wealth of exposed beams' in the low-ceilinged sitting room and a rustic little ladder-stair led up to a bedroom in the tower. With a total overhaul and many, many pounds spent, it could be charm itself.

Maybe, eventually, we could rent it out to discerning tenants who would love the amenity of being able to open the ribbed oak door on a crisp morning and step out into the foothills of Snowdonia. All this passed in a flash through our minds as we surveyed the dingy hovel of a room. The trouble was there was a disquieting permanence to the living quarters as they stood. The Busbys had even rigged up an electricity supply to the main house, the wires of which had sagged to child's height across the gravel. Like it or not, the Busbys were here to stay: hence Peter's 'look on the bright side' palliative as we sat before the fire watching the sparks (given off from the remains of an old hen house) volley up the chimney.

There was nothing in the world I loathed more than a confrontation. I could no more tell the Busbys to go, than I could . . . tell the Busbys to go. And I knew Peter felt the same. I had this nagging feeling in the back of my mind that some antiquated curatorial obligation went with owning a monument such as Gwydir Castle, which insisted that unreasonable access be granted to all comers at any time. It was like owning night or day. Impossible. Ergo, the Busbys had a right to live in the coach house simply because they liked living there.

The easiest way to deal with the problem to our mutual satisfaction was to persuade ourselves that we really did need an electrician. It didn't take much convincing. The sparks which frequently could be heard hissing like a cat from the fuse box in the Hall of Justice had escaped nobody's attention. Sometimes when it rained, the wires fizzed like a test-tube experiment. There was a sporadic supply of electricity to some parts of the house. Often the supply ended on a beam in two lethal wired prongs. A snake of empty white trunking scarred the house as though the money had run out halfway through the job. We'd stripped it out along with the drinks bar on the day of our arrival, as part of the cleansing process. The house felt so much better for it. We'd decided that candles would solely light the main rooms in the castle. Already, with the walls pared of only surface imperfections, the house had space to breathe again. And breathe it did. It began to fill its lungs with its old, lost majesty. It was a thrill to feel. It made me ponder why it was (as I wrenched a defunct fire extinguisher off the wall) that something old and broken had a curious, yet acceptable charm, while something new and broken had no charm at all.

So, we'd survived our first week of castle life and how our bones ached with the triumph of it! We made a decision not to live like foxes in any one part of the house but to spread ourselves around, in an effort to use the castle in the manner for which it had been built. The kitchen, for example, couldn't have been further away from our bedroom, which made the tea run in the morning a bit of an ordeal, especially in winter.

Personally, once I'd got the geography of the house straight in my own mind, I loved the long journey to the kitchen through the Hall of Meredith, down the spiral staircase and across the Lower Hall – I felt it took you through the heart of the house. All the major rooms had at least two doors leading off them which effectively made each room seem like a very large corridor, though the house was built long before the Victorians invented corridors. There were four huge halls, each one capable of holding eighty to a hundred people at a time. But our immediate concerns were more prosaically centred on the smaller rooms in which we proposed to keep warm over the coming winter months. Of these there was a dearth, due to the demolition of the Long Gallery and service wings in the 1820s.

We wandered the empty rooms admiring the tenacity of sagging ceiling plaster and tried in our minds to prioritise the repair work. There was a lot we could do ourselves that

'No comment,' came the reply. He rambled through a programme of repairs as though he were running his finger down a shopping list. The object of the first phase of emergency repair was to make the house wind and watertight and to shore up the chimney stacks that were in imminent danger of collapse. Ultimately, the entire house would need reroofing and all the lead would need replacing; the hard cement pointing from the 1940s would need to be hacked out and replaced with lime pointing, and the bulge in the Solar Tower would need shoring up. And that was just the hors d'oeuvre.

In Graham's opinion there was work enough to give five years' full-time employment to at least five builders. Peter stood in silence for a few moments, trying to do the maths, with a look of utter incomprehension growing on his face.

'Expensive,' broke in Graham, reading our thoughts. Employing five builders for one day, let alone five years was a financial impossibility. No, we told him, we had time on our side, we would pick away at it slowly with one or maybe two builders at most.

'Well, I just hope I live to see it finished,' said Graham, his lips by this time having changed to a fascinating shade of plum purple, 'and if I don't get back to that fire sharpish, I doubt I'll see the rest of the day out.'

The house was quick to give us prizes for our efforts. The first time, it presented us with two initials carved into a chimney stack: the letters IW, and a heart with an arrow through it. We came across this enigmatic cypher as we stripped the ivy from the torso of the hall-range chimney. I wanted to keep the foliage as I couldn't bear the thought of anything that might change the faery look of the house. But even I had to concede that the ivy was doing untold damage to the stonework; it was throttling the life out of the chimneys, it was pulling out the mortar and lifting up the leads. The stripping of the ivy was satisfying work. You started by pulling at a limp tendril that would ultimately lead to a vast latticework of woody stems which would come away in one giant piece, as if the house were shrugging off a great gaberdine of foliage. And, concealed beneath, were the letters carved deep into the granite stone: IW for Iohannes Wynn, John Wynn, put there around 1550 when the stack was built. The heart and arrow remains one of those delicious mysteries that are necessary, if only to confound the experts. The courtyard is frequently rife with speculation: was it some secret Catholic code or was it simply John Wynn telling the world that Gwydir was his heart's delight?

We carefully choreographed the remaining ivy. Not too much, but enough to make you fantasise about Bluebeard's Castle. We allowed it access to the window bars but not the delicate stonework. This was to become the philosophy behind our future restoration of the house. Keeping the faded, slightly crumbling patination of the house intact was absolutely crucial. We would attempt to erase the mistakes of recent renovations and get the house back into health, without losing the romantic appeal of decay and neglect: last summer's swallows' nests, for example, would stay encrusted to the ceiling of the porch; a choice selection of cobwebs would remain to frisk the face unexpectedly in doorways; and all the chandeliers would drip with stalactites of wax. Every room would bear the trace of vanished time – a withered rose, a dead moth, sometimes a bowl of putrefying fruit. But how could I have known then that the house had its own time tricks up its sleeve? And had I known, would that have eased the fright of what was to come?

6

Local Colour

$\mathcal{T}$hey say the road that passes our gate and goes on to Betws-y-Coed is one of the oldest in Wales, pre-Roman, even. It is a beautiful road. It races the river, neck and neck, beneath the scree of conifers which tumble down the Carreg y Gwalch – the Falcon's Rock, where Dafydd ap Siencyn, the Welsh Robin Hood, and his band of men hid out in Edward IV's time. There are stories everywhere among these hills. Stop any local in the street and they will tell you how Dafydd's men were mistaken for fairies in the woods because they wore green and could run like the wind. Approach anyone and they will talk of the monster which lived in a pool upstream from Gwydir beneath a bridge called Pont yr Afanc, the Beaver Bridge. Speak to anyone and they will tell you how Sir John Wynn's tormented soul lies trapped beneath the waters of Rhaiadr y Wennol, the Swallow Falls, having been cursed there for ever by a disgruntled monk for some unrecorded crime against his person. If the night is dark enough and if the wind is in the right direction they say you can hear, above the thrashing crystal waters of the falls, the moans and the wails of his soul trapped in purgatory.

And the Twyleth Teg, the Fairy Folk. They live in the burial chambers and come out at dusk to play among the stones. This is the essence of Wales. So much myth and sorcery the hill people are replete with it, blasé almost. In any number of fields you can stroke the very stone from which Arthur pulled Excalibur and watch the farmer's teasing, elfin face goad you to belief. But watch his hand pat it too when no one's looking – for luck.

It is said that Arthur's men roamed all round these hills looking for grails and Black Knights to slay and dreamy damsels to rescue – the *Mabinogion*, that great Welsh medieval epic, tells us so. Mythology even accords Gwydir its own claim on a Round Table knight – Sir Percival, or Peredur, in Welsh, whose Dark Age fort might well have occupied the rocky plateau above the castle where the chapel now stands.

In the eighteenth century, a German doctor of metals lived at Gwydir. Dr Dietrich Wesel Linden was employed by Lord Willoughby d'Eresby to exploit the mineral deposits in the Gwydir forest. But the folklore of the area overcame him and he spent the next twenty years recording its mythology instead. I have an image of him sitting in a high wing-backed chair, hunched over his books in a draughty chamber somewhere in the castle, writing of the histories, fairies and other oddities of the region.

Gwydir. Its very name has a mystical, grail-like ring to it. Some say the word comes from *gwy tir*, meaning watery land, others say it comes from *gwaed dir*, meaning bloody land, while others say it is simply the literal translation of the Welsh word for glass. Consequently, a dubious legend has arisen that suggests the Wynns were the first in these parts to build a house with glazed windows. Personally, given what we know about the flooding, I'm for the watery land theory.

A building of some kind has stood on this site since the Dark Ages. I have long waited for an adequate explanation as to what exactly was dark about the Dark Ages – given their predilection for illuminating things – but none has been forthcoming. When I think of the Dark Ages I am transported to a place that reminds me of Norway: a country of conifers, longboats and minimal sunshine.

At any rate, a great Dark Age battle was fought on the site of the present house in 610 AD by Llywarch Hen, the Poet Prince, and later in 952 a second battle took place between the sons of Hywel and the Princes Ievan and Iago. The Welsh were always quarrelling with each other, which proved to be their downfall in the end. Had they stopped wasting so much energy fighting among themselves, one feels they might have had a better run at the English.

The last thing of any real significance to have happened in the valley was its sacking in 1468 during the Wars of the Roses. From then on, the towns and villages quietly dozed their way through several centuries, waking up briefly for a royal visit in 1899 and next in 1925 when the village of Dolgarrog was swept away by a flood.

The house sits in a triangle of land a little way out of the town of Llanrwst, its immediate boundaries edged by two minor roads and the river. It was built long before the fashion for driveways and the need for privacy came in. Those Tudors had a different attitude altogether about money – they liked to display, rather than conceal, their wealth. They had none of the social hang-ups we have towards money: if you had it, you made sure you rubbed your neighbour's face in it. Thus the height of your chimneys and the quality of your stockings were a way of advertising the depth of your purse. Without displaying any of the forced self-consciousness of its successors, Gwydir remains a striking landmark across the fields.

In later years, the poetic impact of the Conwy Valley made its mark on many. All the great watercolourists of the eighteenth and nineteenth centuries came and tried to capture the 'pleasing terror' of the scenery. And in their wake, the railway and the tourists arrived, and Betws-y-Coed became what it is today: a holding camp for walkers, day-trippers and amateur artists alike.

The drama of the landscape is a lure to many. The valley sides are as craggy as an old professor's brow. When seen from afar, our Falcon's Rock pushes out into the broad, flat valley like a backdrop in a Wagnerian opera and there we are nestling beneath it, able to taste the heathered air as it glides down on the mountain streams from higher moorland climes.

Some days I would sneak away from the job in hand and spend whole, guilty afternoons driving around in the car, exploring the highways and byways of the valley on the pretext of some errand or other. The car was the only place in which to get really toe-tingling warm. With a dog in the back I'd drive around the high-hedged lanes, the hilltops tugging me higher and higher until I could swear I was on top of the world, with several valleys opening up at my feet and steep drops, sometimes to the left and right, enough to give me vertigo. So high, in fact, I'd attribute my light-headedness to thinning oxygen. I realise now it was love. I was falling in love with a place. It was like pushing through the back of a wardrobe and finding yourself in Narnia. All the creatures up there seemed to be imbued with a kind of otherworldly magic. The buzzard resting on a fence post, disdainful of my presence, with a yellow splinter for a beak peeking out of its sleek, feathered face. And those ghastly talons, flexing and unflexing their grip on the post, in anticipation of the small neck they would shortly close upon. The mountain streams were orange with mineral deposits and when I cupped the ice-cold water to my lips it tasted of iron and bilberries. Sometimes, far off on the opposite slope, a farmer would be gathering his sheep off the mountain. A dog the size of a fly would buzz in wide arcs about the shifting bundle and the farmer on his trike would shout 'cumbye' and 'away', and I would watch transfixed as the dog obeyed and then the sheep reluctantly heeded the dog by filing one by one into the fold of a broken-down wall.

Blasted oaks are a speciality in Wales. You see them everywhere round here. They grow out of the limestone outcrops, rooting down between the broken boulders in nearly-nothing soil; and the stones themselves are covered in cool pillows of moss where Lancelot might have lain his head momentarily in the sun. Any excuse and I would be up there skirting the forestry plantations. The forests are dark places, dark in every sense of the word. They shouldn't be there of course; Sitka spruce is not indigenous to Wales. In the 1920s the land-purloining Forestry Commission cloaked the hills with a harvestable crop, a market force, that drove much of the native flora and fauna away. Nothing likes to live inside these forests. Pennant, the eighteenth-century antiquarian, wrote that the noblest oaks in all of Wales grew on the slopes above Gwydir. But they were all chopped down and someone thought conifers would be a good idea; but they weren't, even if I am a little partial to the eerie light they cast.

Every day there was an errand of some sort to run: into town or the builder's merchant or the baker's. 'I'll go,' we'd all shout, desperate for a session with the car heater, but I usually won as my fingers were always first to fly to the car keys. There was a good ironmonger's in Llanrwst called Jones & Bebb. We practically lived in that shop, stocking up on supplies: buckets and mops and candles by the boxload. It had almost the same allure for me as a stationery shop, with its neat rows of gleaming paint pots, new brushes and packets of seeds. It was deliciously old-fashioned. Sometimes a visit could take anything up to an hour. It was like a slow waltz in blue overalls – everything packaged up so beautifully in brown paper at the end, screws counted, putty wrapped, draw-lining paper unrolled, measured, rerolled. A chat was a prerequisite of being served. My first visit there caused quite a stir. I asked if I could open an account. Glyn Bach, the manager, was summoned from the back of the shop, a man so full of energy he made me feel tired. Bach, of course, was not his real surname; it is Welsh for small, but people rarely go by a real surname in these parts. More often it is some literal anatomical description, or the name of their farm or even their occupation. The opening of an account was an event that required a long search for reading glasses and copious amounts of carbon paper. Eventually, perched on a tall stool, pen poised, he said, 'Address?'

'Gwydir Castle,' I mumbled. I still had trouble relaying my address to people. To be honest I felt a tad unworthy to be, in his eyes, the living representative of such a house.

'What?'

'Gwydir Castle,' I said again, hitching the volume up a notch.

'Gwydir Castle, did you say?'

'Yes,' I smiled self-consciously and rubbed at an invisible mark on the floor with the toe of my shoe.

'Never. Gwynfor, did you hear that? Gwydir Castle's in,' he bellowed across the shop. And Gwynfor arrived fiddling behind his ear with a hearing aid and began to tell me about his aunt who used to work as a guide at the castle in old Mr Clegg's day.

'And how is Sir John Wynn this morning?'

'Fine,' I said quietly.

'Jenny, did you hear that, Gwydir Castle's in?' Jenny came over, lighting up a cigarette, abandoning her line of customers, and told me how as a girl she used to polish the brasses for Mrs Clegg who always made her eat a full roast dinner afterwards. And then some of the customers drifted over because everyone, or so it seemed, had their own story to tell about the castle. Geraint, from the local garage, was standing one night by the bus stop, and looking over our wall into the garden, he saw an old woman dressed in black lace rise out of a ground mist and float across the lawn between the yew trees. 'As clear as gin,' he said.

There were the children who'd played in the burnt-out wings of the house in the '30s and '40s, firing catapults at the stained glass and then walking off with carved heads, door handles and servants' bells. I bet the garden sheds of Llanrwst bulged with Gwydir plunder then, until Aunt Gwladys had a clear-out and that was it – gone. Now, of course, those boys were old men, standing in the Jones &

Bebb queue waiting to be served. One of them told me how an owl had frightened him half to death by flying out of the Great Chamber, almost knocking him down with its great white wings, when at dusk he'd ventured up to the castle alone, for a dare.

Many a garden wall I've peered over in Llanrwst to see an odd stone finial from Gwydir here or there sticking out of a rockery. The finials that decorate our garden walls and parapets are particularly singular, shaped a bit like a spade on a playing card – I'd know them anywhere. The castle, it seemed, was like the river; it wove its slow way through all the locals' lives.

The fire of 1922 was the big local story branded into everyone's memory. Those old men told me how you could see the flames licking out of the Solar Tower for miles around. A coal had rolled out of a fireplace onto a rug and the fire had started. Luckily, if that's the word, the fire had been restricted to the Solar Tower and the north wing by the quick thinking of the local fire brigade who had pumped water from the fountain and doused the flames in time to stop the fire spreading. The rest of the house escaped damage. PC Williams, it was reported in the local papers, cycled over from Llanrwst and rescued the Dowager Countess Tankerville from her smouldering bed and earned himself the credit of local hero for a time.

The Royal Commission came round and took photographs after the fire. Those photographs are harrowing to see. The poor old Solar Tower without a roof, the windows missing, like gouged-out eyes, unseeing, blind, as though some terrible act of torture had been inflicted upon it. It sat empty for twenty years or more, unloved and abandoned, with only the owls for company. Then Arthur Clegg and his wife bought the house and began the task of restoring it. Theirs was an unconventional restoration. They took decisions that we would not take now; but, for certain, they saved the house from ruin. At the time, there were no restrictions on what you could do with an old building, more's the pity. You didn't need permits or listed-building consent to carve up a sixteenth-century post and panel screen – if it got in the way, you just removed it with a saw. The stripping back of subsequent periods to get to the early core of the house was largely down to him, and, consequently, we had an uneasy posthumous relationship with Arthur Clegg: on the one hand he saved the house; on the other he did so much to compromise the historic fabric of the building. He was a product of his age. There was an infernal mania for such stripping out in the '40s and '50s – a kind of Hollywoodian reinvention of history – the bare stone aesthetic, as Peter calls it, which insisted that everyone in the past was two feet tall, had bad teeth and lived in houses with no plaster on the walls. And yet when one looked at the roll-call of great houses that were demolished during the '40s and '50s, Gwydir was a miraculous survival. Arthur Clegg, for all his faults, had seen what we had seen (when others had not): that Gwydir was a building worth making sacrifices for.

A sad, funny story emerged from the ironmonger's queue that said so much about Arthur Clegg's approach to the restoration. There are two dates on either side of the main gate into the courtyard. On the left the date 1555, the date the gate was built, and on the right the date 1828, the date the castle was restored by Lord Willoughby d'Eresby. An oldish man with a corgi touched my arm as I was leaving the shop and told me that cycling past the gates of Gwydir one day he had seen Arthur Clegg up a ladder with a hammer and a chisel, changing the first eight in 1828 to a three. Thus the date now reads 1328!

7

Money-making Schemes

*I*f you want something as badly as we had wanted Gwydir, it's amazing what you can persuade yourself to put up with. Between ourselves we rarely alluded to the discomfort of our living quarters; we were an adaptable pair, I'll say that for us – and determined too. We soon forgot what normal was and settled into our new lives with gusto, laughing at the clumsiness of numb fingers and toes too swollen with chilblains to fit into shoes. Our two lean lurchers felt the cold too. They would jostle for the heat of the fire beneath the faded tapestry we'd nailed to the wall, looking every bit like the goddess Diana's faithful hounds, with their fawn faces tilted to the firelight and their paws deep in a dune of wood ash.

Those first few months of our new lives at Gwydir are grounded in my memory by dishcloths frozen to the draining board, spreadable butter too cold to spread, and the sharp, sheer patterns of ice on the inside of the leaded panes. And in the evenings, sometimes, we'd slope off for an hour to the snug hub of a country inn and feel a glass of cider send a warm glow to our cheeks. And Peter would sketch pen-and-ink reconstructions of how the house might have looked in Sir John Wynn's time. He had such a gift for teasing out the *Zeitgeist* of a house and trapping it on paper. Suddenly, for the place to be transformed by the swirl of a pencil: gabled dormers reinstated, gardens neatly tended; it was indeed tantalising to see what a difference four million pounds or so could bring about.

It was the only time we ever had to be alone. Since news had reached the outside world that the new young owners of Gwydir Castle had taken up residence, the house had become like a mainline station at rush hour. Friends, well-wishers and snoopers alike flocked for a private view. It felt a little like living inside a display cabinet where all kinds of enquiring fingers came and poked around and turned us over for a better look. Sometimes we'd come down and find the kitchen bursting with people. There might be the Busbys, their offspring and friends, as well as Sven and perhaps a couple of strangers who had found their way into the house and had been offered refreshment by Jerry, who was brewing up tea in the middle of it all.

What, in fact, we craved most was to be left alone to get on with making the house semi-presentable before people were invited into it. Squalor only becomes difficult to cope with when other people see you living in it. There was something indelicate about it; something akin to being caught in a state of undress.

We had a beautiful, ancient bell at the gate, irresistible to small children, but seemingly not to adults. It was an old copy of a Celtic bell that looked a bit like a cowbell with a piece of rope attached to its inside which, when pulled, made the clapper clonk discordantly. No one ever bothered to announce their arrival by pulling it. For some reason the whole world and his wife, and her aunts and their nephews, all treated Gwydir as though it were a public park. They would just open the gate and come straight in. No matter what you were doing, there they would be: total strangers, head round the door. 'Do you sell thimbles?' was the best opening line I ever heard. Another good one was 'Just curious to know how much you paid for the old wreck.' Such a shameless question deserved a curt response.

Early one morning as I emerged sleepily into the Hall of Meredith, I heard voices floating up between the floorboards. It was too early for the rest of the household, which had established a pattern of starting late and finishing late. Still in my pyjamas, with tousled hair, and muffled up to the eyeballs in scarves and mittens, I slithered down the spiral staircase and there before me in the Lower Hall were a group of Japanese tourists taking pictures of one another in front of the fireplace. I rubbed my eyes. They must have got in through one of the many doors that wouldn't lock.

'No, no, no,' I said, in what I thought was a fairly disapproving tone. They all turned towards me and I became instantly aware of what I must have looked like to them. Reflected in the bank of camera lenses, I saw the very vision of Mr Rochester's mad attic wife.

'Good morning, how do you do?' came the immaculate Baedeker response from the tour leader. And then the barrage of lenses began to fire and flash, making me feel like some grim parody of a catwalk model. Amidst much clucking and general confusion I shooed them back out the way they had come. The tour leader said, 'It is disappointing, no, that you do not have a gift shop.' I winced at the gall of it, but at the same time the light bulb of an idea had gone off in my head.

The Busbys, meanwhile, were living like kings in the coach house compared to us, though I didn't begrudge them their comfort as Jim had already proved himself invaluable by getting the old boiler going in our quarters. Three bursts and two floods later Peter turned on the tap and held his breath. The wheezing system spat out air and then shuddered into life and coughed out a trickle of hot water. Had liquid gold flowed from those taps I couldn't have been more delighted. A five-minute traipse to the kitchen to boil the kettle for a wash in the morning was now a thing of the past. No more cold licks with a damp flannel but a proper soak in a tub, albeit a pink, plastic tub (a 1970s refugee) but a tub nevertheless. For hours at a time I luxuriated in the pure bliss of this simple pleasure.

Every day we learnt a little more about the house and the more familiar it became, the more, if it was possible, we grew to love it. In Sir John Wynn's day, forty servants had run the house; now there were but two of us. There was just no time for our respective jobs, and to be honest, no inclination either; demanding mistress that she was, the house commanded our full and focused attention. And gradually the rooms began to sing again. Mercifully, there was rarely any discord about what needed to be done. To us it was blatantly obvious how each room ought to look, and with this clear vision fixed firmly in our minds we worked steadily towards our goal. Looking back, I can see that had the degree of compulsion been unequal between us the whole enterprise may never have got off the ground. As it was, we were in complete accord and our joint determination created the momentum to propel our labours forward.

We polished up the old oak floorboards and improvised on long refectory tables with Turkish carpets thrown over trestles and scaffolding planks. We hung antlers above inglenooks and hid the wounds in the stonework with brocade hangings. Even the kitchen was now marginally habitable and the thought of associating raw food with this room was no longer nauseating. Every little broken square of glass had been replaced in the windows and the wind no longer prowled through the house at night. The rats, too, were on the wane and two kittens with impeccable mousing pedigrees had been procured. They arrived in a box with the words 'Grappolino Oranges' on the side. They were henceforth known as the Grappolino twins.

And then the day came, as it must always come, when the few hundred pounds we had left to our names had dwindled to approximately thirty-seven pence. It was a shock to the system, I can tell you. Not that it had happened: it was inevitable that we would run out of money at some point, but that it had happened so soon, that was the shock.

'It's all very well having ideals, but ideals won't pay the bills,' my visiting mother considerately reminded us, as she delivered the third food parcel of the week. Truth be told, both Peter and I had secretly hoped that something would just come out of the woodwork and save us – a rich, philanthropic benefactor, for example, who would look upon our struggle to restore this great house with sympathy and, ultimately, benevolence. As it happened, something did not so much come out of the woodwork as out of the woods. A ten-pound note in fact. I found it lying there on Lady Mary's Walk, the path that leads down to the castle from the chapel. I'd paused on the path with the dogs as I always did on my daily walks through the wood. The view of the house from up here was a great favourite of mine. The vast spread of buildings and the dozen tall chimneys rising out of a jumble of roof reminded me of Tennyson's knight riding down to 'many tower'd Camelot'. Beyond, in the garden, a thin river mist lingered in the hollows. My eyes wandered from the house and fell to the ground, and there at my feet was a ten-pound note resting on a pile of humus and decaying laurel leaves. At first I thought it was some floating mirage come to trick my senses, but when I looked again it was still there. I picked it up and though the leaves it had nestled among were wet with dew, the note was perfectly dry and crisp, as though it had only moments ago been ejected from a cash dispenser.

There was magic in the air! I had the strangest feeling that the ten-pound note was a portent. A portent that all would be well if we could find it in ourselves to have absolute trust in the sublime hand that had, after all, led us to this place.

'You won't believe what's happened,' said Peter. He was waiting at the gate as I came down from the hill.

'I bet I will,' I replied.

'If I told you a London PR firm had just telephoned and offered us five thousand pounds for the use of Gwydir for a fashion shoot, you wouldn't believe me, would you?'

'You're right, I wouldn't,' I said.

'Well, it's true. As true as that chimney stack over there.' I eyed the sickle-shaped stack with suspicion. 'Five days at a thousand pounds a day! We can start on the roof, we can hire the scaffolding, we can do the chimneys . . . ' He was off, ferried far away on a raft of hopeful optimism, and by the time he'd finished that five thousand pounds had been made to stretch right round the house and back again.

In the kitchen a week later, Peter announced, 'If this tea bag goes into that mug, the fashion shoot will happen.' It was a ridiculous game we'd started playing which had evolved into a kind of obsession, like avoiding the cracks in the pavement or waving at magpies. The rules were you took three long strides away from the kettle and then tried to throw the tea bag into the mug. It was not the enjoyment of the game that appealed so much to us; it was the utter puerility of it that would often see us convulsed with laughter, tears streaming down our cheeks as the eighteenth throw missed its target.

'No, really, listen,' said Peter, 'if I get this one in, the fashion shoot will go ahead.' The PR company had been back in touch several times. The deal was almost sealed. The shoot would consist of twenty-five people including three models and five technicians. They wanted Arthur Clegg's rugged, bare-stone look, would you believe, the Fred Flintstone look. A hush fell across the kitchen. Peter played the moment, rolling up his sleeves and taking aim like a veteran dart player. He threw the tea bag and it bounced off the edge of the mug and fell into a small puddle of milk and sugar grains, just to the left of the kettle.

The telephone rang. 'It's them,' Peter said, with his hand over the receiver. 'Yes . . . right . . . of course. Any time you like . . . Oh, by the way, just out of interest, what sort of fashion is it?' We'd forgotten to ask in the excitement of it all. Long pause and the hint of a frown on Peter's brow. A longer pause followed, of the kind that usually heralds the arrival of a fairly large disappointment.

'Women's fashion, you say. What do you mean: "tasteful" ' He said, 'I see,' in a way that made me think he didn't see at all. 'Can I get back to you in an hour? Good. We'll talk then. Thanks. Bye.' And then, turning to me, 'You won't believe this.'

'D'you know, you're right, I bet I won't,' I said, with no surprise in my voice this time.

The London PR firm turned out to be representing a well-known company which specialised in sex aids and 'tasteful' lingerie (if such a thing existed outside the Damart thermal vest range which I'd become very partial to indeed). The plan was to shoot their new catalogue of leather wear at Gwydir. After digging around a bit, we discovered that 'leather wear' was a tatty little euphemism for bondage and some other activity which I thought was illegal in most decent European countries. Old-fashioned we might be, but as far as appearances went, we felt that 'Fetish Fantasy in Feudal Fortress' headlines would do us no good at all. Gwydir's seedy nightclub image was taking a long time to die down. The booming house music of June's day still rang loud in the town's ears and the local constabulary were no strangers to the Great Chamber. And so it came to pass that we turned whatever it is you're supposed to turn (perhaps a cheek) when the devil tempts, and with righteous hearts we bade adieu to the five thousand pounds.

Here ends the first lesson. Never spend five thousand pounds unless you have it in your back pocket. In fairness, we hadn't actually spent the five thousand pounds; it was more we'd spent the promise of it. We'd had a week of interviewing builders and these builders were split very firmly into two camps. There were the builders Graham, our architect, had sent: the clean overalls and polished ladders type. And then there were the builders we'd found ourselves through the hillside grapevine, so to speak. There was a natural incentive to try to keep all costs to an absolute minimum. Large firms of contractors had overheads – they had Thermos flasks to fill, they had new vans to service, they had VAT returns to complete. That wasn't what we wanted at all. New-build contractors jarred with the spirit of the house. They knew how to build a breeze-block extension or put up a conservatory, but most of them had never worked with lime before. They had never felt the slop of mortar slide off their trowels onto a wall five hundred Christmases old.

And then one day in walks Will Pierce. Or more precisely, the odour of sheep arrives first and then the man. It's a smell I know well: a good wedge of my childhood was spent on a farm, in the lambing shed. The smell of him takes me right back there, to the muck and milk and afterbirth. The heady mixture is smeared right down the front of his trousers. It bears the glazed consistency of dried egg. Numerous pieces of straw stick out of his thick thatch of tight black curls, and yet when he smiles, I see beneath the layer of topsoil a man of cherubic Celtic beauty. He is short, stocky: the archetypal Welshman. And he's not a man for mincing words either. 'Stacks. I've come to see the chimney stacks.' His accent is as broad as it gets, that lovely Caernarvonshire lilt, so different from the south, more rounded, as if bubbles come out with the words. He reaches down inside his jumper and pulls out a plastic pouch of tobacco. Take your seats, ladies and gentlemen, please, the Ceremony of the Roll-up is about to begin. I watch transfixed as a heaped line of tobacco is placed upon the tissue-thin sheet of Rizla. The rolling begins between thumb and forefinger and then a semi-erotic interchange takes place between the edge of the paper and the tip of his tongue. With a twirl, the tobacco is ensnared like a body in a rolled-up carpet. Loose shreds are tapped away and the moment when industry reaps its reward finally arrives. He puts the smoke to his lips, cups his hands around a match to get a light and draws deeply, narrowing his eyes just slightly, savouring the hit at the back of his throat. He is clearly not a man to be rushed.

'I'll get Peter,' I say and offer him tea. He nods. No word of thanks, just a nod, brusque-like. Again, I watch transfixed as he stirs four heaped spoonfuls of sugar into his tea. He is a Betws-y-Coed man, lived there all his life on the same farm, with four brothers and a matriarchal mother who, by all accounts, ruled them with a rod of willow. The farm, which is still on the old Gwydir estate, is called Bod Gethin, Gethin's Place, after Rhys Gethin who was Owain Glyndwr's lieutenant at the turn of the fifteenth century.

Will, we subsequently learn, is the secretary of the Betws-y-Coed Fox Destruction Society – no scented drawer-lining to that name, straight to the point, like its secretary. Strange reference, but it serves. It becomes clear that what he knows best is buildings – and old buildings at that.

'The men who built this house knew a thing or two about working with stone,' he says. When he can't find the English word, he lapses into Welsh, and when you hear the ancient rhythms of his language it is not difficult to imagine that the men who built this house might well have been his ancestors. His hands are as cracked as a parched riverbed. He has grown out of this landscape like a tree that turns its back against the wind and grows in spite of itself.

The ultimate test: Peter extracts a small lump of original mortar from his pocket. No one yet has been able to tell us what the mystery ingredient is, the small shards of aggregate, which bind the mixture together, though Peter has a hunch. Will crumbles it between his fingers, lifts it to his nose, breaks it into dust. 'Two lime, four sand, three grit,' he says without hesitation.

'And the grit, where does the grit come from?' we ask together.

'From the river here, of course. Gower's Pool probably.' That clinches it for us. Peter's hunch was right. A man who can pinpoint the right river, let alone the exact pool the river grit comes from, must be worth his salt. I take a peek at my watch and realise we've been talking for two hours. He might not mince his words but he loves to talk. Talk the hind legs off a donkey as the cliché goes, and takes everything nice and slowly, one word, sure-footedly, in front of the other, as though he has a huge mountain to climb and he's pacing himself. And all is punctuated by a periodic 'Bloody whatdyacallit,' when the English fails him.

'So when could you start on the chimneys?' we ask.

He lights another roll-up. Picks a stray piece of tobacco from his tongue. 'In a while,' he says, 'when my sheep have finished lambing.'

By the time our search for the right people has ended, we find ourselves surrounded by a splendid array of lovable misfits, all mavericks in their own way: moody, maverick artisans. Syd the Roofer, for example, and his sidekick, the Scouse Git, the only name he answers to. Now Syd might have graced any French salon at the turn of the century with confidence. His refined features and pale countenance gave him the look of a consumptive on a damp day. His blond, lanky hair reached down to his shoulders and he had the hands of a pianist, his fingers thin and grey like river weed. We had seen his work elsewhere on chapel roofs and it was good. It was *sympatique*. He spoke of the house in awe-hushed tones as though he was afraid of offending it. But the question was, would he live to see the job through? He had this hacking cough which sent his body into convulsions when it started, and these sessions would go on for ages until he emerged as though out of a tunnel, dark-eyed and silent. I felt he needed smelling salts and a *chaise longue*, not a castle roof on a cold January day. An untipped cigarette always brought him round. He was as good as new after a long, deep draw.

And then there was Dave the Scaffolder, ex-sergeant in the Paras and a Falklands veteran: built like the proverbial.

He spoke in a throttled bass whisper that made the tendons in his bullish neck tense and tremble like plucked harp strings. It was the voice of someone more used to shouting than talking. I don't quite know why I should feel so fondly towards him, since it was obvious he didn't much like women. When he first arrived at the gate, he looked over my head and asked to speak to the boss. Imagine how well that went down. I think it was the tenderness he showed towards his small son that made me stick with him; the care with which he took the child's hand in his own massive, shovel-sized hand without inadvertently crushing the small bones to a pulp. For some reason, it made me think I might have mistaken chauvinism for shyness. Anyway, he agreed with Peter to scaffold the west wing and the two worst chimneys. The scaffolding went up the following day and it was so heartening to see it there finally. It made us feel that things were really happening at last; that we were making progress, that apparently we had absolutely everything under control.

Though we'd been trying hard, above the din, to 'listen to our inner selves', we still hadn't found a solution that would stave off our impending destitution and pay the workmen's wages. But the impromptu visit from the Japanese that morning had sown the seed of an idea that had begun to germinate into something bigger. Supposing we were to open the house to the public again, as it had been in the '60s and '70s? Given that a large proportion of the western hemisphere already appeared to have beaten a path to our door, the logical extension of this was that the remaining proportion would be prepared to pay for the privilege of doing likewise. OK, so the house might, in part, be a roofless ruin, but so was every other ancient monument in Wales you paid money to see. And in its day Gwydir had apparently attracted 50,000 visitors or so! Yes, that was it. We'd put a sign up at the gate announcing that the castle was open to the public during its restoration. We would close off those parts of the house that were just too dangerous to visit. We would only open on days when it wasn't raining, as the buckets were apt to make the place look untidy. We would produce a leaflet, perhaps a guidebook even, and people could wander at a leisurely pace through the deserted rooms. And just to be on the safe side, we would erect a large 'Enter At Your Own Risk' sign in case anyone decided to take a tumble through a hole in the floor.

How hard would it be to share our home with strangers? This thought did, for a time, stalk restlessly round my mind, barging and prowling into areas marked private. It was not an easy thought to bear, but our hands were bound by necessity. This home, in particular, was sanctuary writ large. How would anyone feel inviting the murderer, the thief, the assassin into one's sacred space – and worse: the solicitor or the accountant? 'Be not neglectful to entertain strangers for thereby some have entertained angels unawares,' came the admonishment from on high. The noble thought entered my head that if one single mortal could find solace here at Gwydir from the madness of modern life, then it would be worth all the inconvenience in the world.

At the end of a fortnight, the house was still dangerous

but at least it was decent. All the remaining rubbish had been cleared from the rooms, or at least cleared away into the rooms that would be hidden from the hordes of people we were anticipating.

However seductive the thought, an instant 'abracadabra!' transformation was not possible in the garden. We gave it our best, though: we cleared the weed trees from around the house and the light sprang in through the windows; we clipped and we pruned and beat back the rampant growth from the paths, and we hauled the old Hayter mower to and fro across the patch of scutch grass that served as a stretch of lawn closest to the house. We mowed paths through the remaining wilderness to make it look as though we knew what we were doing.

At some point under June's management, forty tons of crushed road had been spread all over the courtyard, probably bought as a cheap lot from some itinerant council worker who was looking for somewhere to offload the scrapings of the old A470. Bits of crushed yellow lines were sprinkled like confetti around the courtyard and the cats eyes could catch you by surprise at night if you caught them in the beam of a torch. Sven shovelled the worst off before spreading the new gravel that accentuated the delicate shades of buff in the sandstone window-surrounds. He worked methodically, pacing himself like a well-schooled shire horse; unlike the rest of us who charged into jobs and burnt ourselves to a near crisp of exhaustion within the hour.

Only the other night we'd found ourselves passing Sven's caravan. We peered in through the gauzed window and there he sat, this big man shoehorned into his plyboard hutch, hunched over a book, looking in the lurid light of the unshaded bulb like St Jerome, with the ascetic's shaven head, the faraway look, the scattered papers. I'd found him, just the day before, weeping in the garden over a nest of baby hedgehogs he'd disturbed with his shovel while digging out some old root or other. I couldn't bring myself to intrude on his grief which, something told me, went far beyond the hedgehogs; I felt he wanted silence. There were unfathomable depths to Sven who was, in every regard, one part Prospero, one part Caliban. We often shared a beer with him in the evening. His jangled nerves relaxed after a beer and he became almost comprehensible.

'Where did you get those scars?' we asked him as the midges feasted on our ankles.

'Bottled in Bergen,' he said, pointing to a pale stripe down the side of his nose.

'And that one, Sven, where did you get that one?'

'Knifed by a shipmate in Marseilles.' His voice ran on through a macabre litany of beatings sustained during the twenty years of his life as an able seaman in the Merchant Navy.

'I had to get out in the end,' he said. 'That's why I'm here.' So Gwydir had become a sanctuary for him, too. He was healing in the silence of the garden.

Most nights we would take a stroll (or sometimes a weary stagger) round the garden to view the day's achievements. I loved it at night. Not that I loved it less during the day. But to walk in the moon-washed shadows of the yew trees and to see the ancient profile of the house silhouetted against a cloudless sky was to feel oneself suspended out of time, as though in that moment we were living in parenthesis. Sometimes, if the night was cold enough, the trails of yesterday's peacock tails would be cast in frost across the patches of lawn we had managed to scythe the day before. Lingering for a moment beneath Sir John Wynn's arch, from which worn steps led down into the Dutch Garden, you could see the lumps and bumps in the lawn below – more pronounced somehow in the moonlight – that denoted an earlier path, or perhaps a terrace or an ancient planting line. We would walk down to the bottom of the garden and sit on the massive slate bench, looking back up the avenue of yew trees towards the house, with the secret sounds of the night rustling and chirruping around us.

A frequent topic of conversation as we sat lingering in the moonlight was how best to present the house to the public. Years of exhaustively visiting National Trust properties had shown us what we did not want Gwydir to become. It was a home, not a museum, a tea room or a shop. There was unanimity between us, as there was in all things aesthetic. To us, the most enriching visitor experience was afforded by those houses still lived in by a family. The least successful, in our eyes, was the themed historical stage set. We vowed there would be no ropes at Gwydir, no harrying stewards or headphone tours. We wanted people to engage fully with the atmosphere: the crackle of the fire, the cry of the peacocks, the scent of candle grease and wood smoke were as much a part of the experience as engaging with the architecture. Heady principles to adopt, given the state of the house, you might think, but it was a template for the future, an ideal to aim for.

Gwydir had a long history of being open to the public. In the nineteenth century, the visiting traveller could pay a small gratuity to the resident Scottish housekeeper in return for being shown 'the old state rooms of the house'. At the turn of the century, a guidebook noted that the castle was 'open when the Earl of Carrington is not in residence. 12–5 daily, Sundays excepted (fee optional)'.

When Arthur Clegg had completed his restoration after the fire, he too opened Gwydir to the public. I am told that was when I first visited the house as a child, in 1973. I can remember nothing of the house, but I do remember the assortment of wildfowl in the garden for which you could buy corn in the gift shop, and I remember the cry of the peacocks which was the saddest sound I'd ever heard. We have guidebooks from that period. It shows the house eclectically furnished with lion's head rugs on the floor and mahogany dining tables laid for dinner. It looks very 1973: not 1573 or even 1673, as you would expect. Any trace of the ancient house had vanished beneath a pall of pleated lampshades.

8

In Camera

We waited. We waited in an ever-dwindling ecstasy of anticipation. It was February. The weather was still cold and grew colder still. The halls rang with a hollow silence. It was like living inside a clapperless bell. Who on earth, out of choice, would visit a country house in February we asked by way of consolation. Every other ancient building in the area was closed up for the season; the very countryside appeared to be resting beneath a dust sheet before the spring onslaught of foot and cycle. The notebook I'd bought to keep a record of visitor numbers sat with unbroken spine next to the unopened bills.

But we were lucky. We were very lucky indeed. Peter had thrown a tea bag from the far end of the kitchen and this time it had ricocheted off the handle of the kettle and had fallen into the mug. It was an unheard of achievement and it meant our luck was about to change for real this time. We waited. And while we waited, Peter, egged on by Sven and Jerry, developed a craze for opening fireplaces. It was definitely a boy's thing and fell into the same category as the search for priests' holes and secret hiding places where the jewels might have been stashed. For didn't every old house have a hidden jewel story? Just as every old house had a story to tell of Queen Elizabeth I who had supposedly slept 'in this very bed'. You couldn't help but get swept up in the general enthusiasm of the search. The trouble was the first exploratory thwack of the claw hammer committed us to at least a week's hard labour and a week of soot, plaster dust, rubble removal and jackdaws' nests. There was a large fireplace in the kitchen to be opened. You could hear it hollow behind a stud and plasterboard wall, presumably erected at the same time as the flagstones were covered over with a skin of concrete.

The first thwack of the claw hammer burst through the plasterboard and a down draught of air sent a mushroom cloud of soot into the room. Right on cue, our less than sonorous bell sounded at the gate. The first time it had sounded in over two weeks, in fact, since the sign announcing we were open daily to the public had gone up. The kitchen was slightly below ground level. It had the air of a burrow and it was dark enough to warrant a candlelit breakfast even if the sun was shining. Had someone been minded to peer in through the window at that moment, six pairs of eyes would have floated before them out of the gloom like night-lights. Our faces were boot-brush black from the fall of soot; we were black from top to toe.

Outside in the courtyard a volley of people swarmed. We spied on them through the leaded panes. There were people in oversized, fluorescent puffer jackets who clutched moble phones to the sides of their heads as though nursing sore ears. There were people with clip-boards, light meters, camcorders and every other cinematic gadget imaginable.

A quick wipe-down with that frozen dishcloth and we were as good as new.

'Think tea bag,' Peter said, as we went out and intro-duced ourselves to the location manager.

'Nice place you've got here,' he said.

'Isn't it,' we said meekly.

Fumbling with his glasses, he said, 'Now, we're here because we're looking for a place to film X. It's a sort of period drama, murder mystery – you know the sort of thing?' We did. 'It's the story of the Earl of Leicester who supposedly did in his wife by pushing her down the stairs so he could free himself up to marry Liz I. This is ideal,' he added, casting a hand towards the house, 'just what we're looking for . . .'

Bingo! This was the start of something big, as they say in Hollywood.

'We've got a tiny budget to work with,' he said.

'Not as tiny as ours,' we assured him.

The magic figure of five thousand pounds was offered and was accepted without demur. We shook hands enthusiastically. Filming was to start almost immediately. Oh blessed tea bag! We could have whooped for joy.

'And *action*.' It was hard to believe in this shape-shifting world of cameras and lights that they still shouted out the old cliché. But there it was. The cameras whirred and the whole room held its breath as lines were spoken, as cleavages heaved, as peacocks screamed and interrupted the shot.

'Cut,' someone shouted.

'F''ing hell,' breathed the leading lady, who was dressed in the rich robes of an Elizabethan lady of some substance. A modern maidservant took the opportunity to rush up and dab at her nose with a powder puff. 'Shoo,' she said, adapting to her role of spoilt miss with unsurprising ease.

We were three days into the shoot. The experience of

having a film crew in the house felt something akin to standing in the middle of an ice rink while a very rowdy game of ice hockey was going on around you. On the first day, we opened the door of the Solar Tower and in they all rushed like a tidal wave: froth of Lycra, spume of fluorescent colour, splashing the flagstones with coffee as a swell of electrical cables broke on the threshold. The outlay of energy was prodigious. I couldn't help thinking of the alternative uses we could have put this resource of manpower to; what wonders we could have created with a tenth of their budget: the gardens, gazebos, the lovely painted chambers we could have made.

We watched bemused as a perfectly authentic Tudor interior was skilfully turned into a fake Tudor interior. We dallied beneath bowers of armoured cabling. We were trodden underfoot by the throng of extras, make-up ladies, 'best boys', 'grips', 'sparks', who charged about the house like darts. We were caught in the crossfire of gaffer tape and aerosol cans. The Styrofoam cup was the symbol of all this.

There were moments of beauty, though, away from the cameras. The sight of an extra for example – one in particular, who had a good period face: thin, pale, poetic-looking, a young Sir Philip Sidney perhaps, who I saw striking an attitude with his back to me beneath Sir John's arch. I did a double take. It was so uncanny and so very right. The arch responded like a stroked cat. It made me hate my modern clothes. But then he turned and I saw it was not an attitude he was striking after all. He was making a call on his mobile phone, expressing his point with his free hand. The image cracked and shattered into a thousand tiny pieces.

Back inside, a set designer attacked a candelabrum with a blowtorch to get that dripped-wax effect. 'Like the candles you have upstairs,' he said enviously. 'Can we hire your cobwebs, by the way?'

The generator wagons growled and grumbled from morning till night, feeding the lights that blasted the house, illuminating the rot, the sags and our fraying nerves.

'No, you *cannot* use my very, very rare Elizabethan coffer as a prop,' I heard Peter shout from the Great Chamber. 'And even if you had had the courtesy to ask, I wouldn't have let you.' Meanwhile I was busy arranging for a local farmer to come and tow a six-ton lighting lorry off our lawn that should not have been there in the first place. Wheels span, mud flew, it was like a wet day at an agricultural show. And there were other misdemeanours: the marauding urinators, for example, those extras who were ferried in by bus in the evening to play the rowdy rabble. They had been plied with lager on the coach to get them in the mood, and they were in the mood all right: laughing and joking and slapping my back; not funny. They were too lazy, too drunk, too . . . to walk the short distance to the car park where the small village of portable amenities resided. So they went outside and relieved themselves against the walls of the gatehouse. The last straw. If my memory serves me right, I think the word 'savage' was used in remonstration.

The following morning it was our turn to feel chastened. The props department had spent the previous day creating a banquet scene of Hampton Court proportions. There were hogs' heads and devilled dishes and specially baked sweetmeats sent up from London. Half the shot had been filmed; it was a welcome-home scene for the prodigal master himself. It was getting late. The cameramen were looking at their watches, continuity were stage-whispering about union rules.

'Cut. We'll pick up where we left off tomorrow,' yelled production. Finally, the generators were unplugged and never had silence seemed so loud or darkness seemed so deep, so total. In the middle of the night, the Grappolini twins and our two lean lurchers made for the room full of Turkish delight . . . What wonders were before them; what miracles of culinary science had been created for their delectation. It was easy to imagine those four furry faces pausing on the threshold of their crime like children, spoilt for choice, standing before a mound of Christmas presents. Which one first? But our brood was not so discerning. They took the whole lot on at once. They jumped up on the table and waded in, galosher-style. And what fun they had! What a triumph of excess they wreaked. Later, having chomped their way through half a pig, a side of beef, any number of dainty pastries, and a syllabub or two, they slunk back to bed, stomachs bulging as though a weather balloon had been sewn inside each of their pelts.

The nocturnal gorge naturally lead to sickness, diarrhoea and vomiting, and all was redeposited across the floorboards of the Great Chamber the following morning. It was there in full, glorious technicolour for the entire cast to see, as was the scene of culinary carnage.

What could we say to the props department except 'these things happen', and 'you know what they say, never work with children or animals'? Eyebrows were raised but there were few laughs.

The great coup occurred the following night. Again it was late, later than usual. The shoot was over-running and Lord Leicester's courtiers were anxious to slip out of their codpieces and make last orders at the Pen-y-Bont.

'Cut. Thank you, ladies and gentlemen, see you eight thirty sharp for the bedroom scene,' said the director and there was the usual stampede towards the door. Generators were silenced, catering wagons locked up for the night, Portaloos abandoned in a state of blocked hopelessness. But in the general mêlée of departure they forgot to take the keys out of the cherry picker. Now, a cherry picker is a very useful machine. In the words of the man who delivered it, it was 'an expensive bit of kit'. It consisted of a small bucket on the end of a great big mechanical arm that could hoist you up sixty or seventy feet or so into the air. We'd had our eye on it for a few days, watching, waiting, biding our time. I plugged a floodlight into the one solitary socket we possessed in the house and the empty stage was lit. It made you feel nostalgic for the greasepaint. Peter and Jerry climbed into the basket of the cherry picker.

'Now, how do we use this thing?' said Peter, pulling levers and pressing knobs at random.

'Let's try the ignition first, shall we?' said Jerry. And suddenly they were off, jerked into the air by the steely thrust of the metal arm. 'Whoa, steady on,' cried Jerry, as though he were calming a recalcitrant stallion. And away they went: up, down, sideways, forwards, just missing the house with inches to spare. They began to climb, higher and higher, zigzagging their way sixty feet up, to the top of the gable-end chimney stack. This was our chance to remove the sycamore saplings that had rooted between the crenellations surmounting the tallest stack and generally do some serious roof gardening.

All was going to plan until – my heart ceased to beat, my mouth went dry – I saw what was happening on the ground. The platform from which the arm was raised began to tip forward. The weight of the men in the bucket, so high, with the arm extended to its fullest limit, was proving too much for the counterbalancing properties of the platform. Jim, too, saw what was happening and immediately threw himself onto the platform. I followed suit, but our combined featherweights could not bring the platform back down to rest on terra firma. There was a moment of suspended animation while we yelled and shrieked for help. There was only one person who could save us now. There was only one person whose ample frame could bring the platform back down to earth. Curious to see what all the noise was about, Jim's wife homed into view. When she saw what was happening, she came thundering from the house and launched herself at the platform. Salvation! With a redistribution of weight, the platform swayed in the balance and then rocked softly back into its cradle. The clonk of metal sent the peacocks screeching. Any loud mechanical sound set them off. It was hard to imagine there was any more screech left in them after the racket of the filming.

We sat leaning against the cherry picker like battle-weary soldiers, the adrenalin giving way to relief. A thin, frightened voice floated down from above 'Do you think we could come down now?' We looked up and saw eight white knuckles clamped to the side of the raised bucket and Jerry's ashen face peeping out between. I am ashamed to say that a really mean part of myself found his perturbation very amusing indeed.

9
Testing Times

I'm restless tonight; can't sleep for trying. Those time tricks I mentioned earlier come next in the chain of events that is our story here and it makes me nervous. I vowed I would never go back to that place. I locked those awful memories in a box marked 'Don't Drink' and threw away the key. But here I am about to shake the box, to make the memories come tumbling out of the slit in the top. I considered skipping this part, but to cut out the heart of my story made me feel like a backstreet surgeon, in some squalid basement, about to perform an illegal operation. I just can't do it; it wouldn't be honest, wouldn't be true, if I just focused on the happy bits.

Appropriate that I should choose the dead of night to conjure up her face again or that the dead of night should choose me. The house is as silent as the grave. Earlier, I took a restless walk around the rooms with a lighted candle before I settled down to write – just to be sure there was nothing lurking in the corners of my mind, as there had been once before. The house was full of the perfumes of the night. I was afraid of nothing. The only fright I had was when the bats came out in a rush from the priest's hole and brushed the air around my face. It was like being fanned with pieces of old, decaying vellum.

It sounds so brash, so unsubtle to say the house is haunted, was haunted. I'm not sure which now. There were no spooks in sheets or rattling chains; our girl was too beguiling in her art, too aware of the beautiful moment to resort to gimcrack tricks.

It started when we began unblocking the fireplace in the

Royal Bedroom, so called because the future King George V and Queen Mary had slept there in 1899, as guests of the Earl of Carrington. But now it was a room that spoke more of the 1940s: fake-beamed, pub-style ceiling; raised patio-pointing around the exposed stones of the walls and a tiny, crazy-paved fireplace; fine for suburbia *circa* 1942 but not for a castle that depended on the bigness of everything. It was like false teeth that didn't fit; it was hideous, it was awful and it had to go. Peter and I stood back and allowed the 'experts' (Will and Sven) to wield the sledgehammers. As usual, Arthur Clegg's mortar mix put up a fight. It was heavy on the cement, light on sand, and the thwacks reverberated around the house until finally the binding, granite-like mixture surrendered and released its bounty of heavy stones.

Then it happened. Just as Sven was removing the last stone I saw Peter fall forward towards the fireplace. I thought at first some noxious gas had been released from the opening which had rendered Peter insensible, but it wasn't a swooning kind of fall, it was more of a violent stumble, as though he had been pushed forward from behind. Breath was held. I watched it happen in slow motion, and again many times later the repeat play of the thwarted accident. Had he not thrown out his arms in time, he might have dashed his head on the ragged stones jutting from the fireplace. Mercifully, it was an accident foiled by his own quick reflexes.

'What are you playing at?' he said, throwing me a hurt, quizzical look.

'You don't think *I* . . . ?' My voice trailed like the tail of a kite. 'Do you? How could I have pushed you, I was standing right in front of you?'

A bewildered look passed over his face as he tried to comprehend what had happened. He said he'd felt a hand on his shoulder pushing him forwards with enormous strength. Will and Sven were kneeling before the fireplace, oblivious. There was nobody else in the room and the temperature had plummeted, as though some chill, Arctic wind had blown the window open.

And that was the start of it. Why then? I have pondered 'why then, why us?' a hundred times, maybe even more. I have heard that building work can sometimes disturb the spirits of a house but I knew in my heart that our discerning spirits were delighted, as we were, that the ugly fire-surround was finally being removed. Knowing what I know now, I am inclined to believe that it had more to do with Peter having proposed to me the night before.

'Let's make an honest woman of the house,' he'd said over baked beans and whisky – for the night was especially cold. And we'd laughed because marriage seemed somehow so irrelevant to our lives. But I'd said yes, thinking that once we'd got it over with we could be left alone to get on with the rest of our lives. Always the pragmatist, me. It must be said, we were both little interested in the bother of a wedding: it would merely serve to take us away from the task in hand, that of restoring the house. We were bound to each other already in every possible way. There had not been a love in either of our lives to match the kindred nature of our journey together. It was for ever.

We'd been planting yew trees the previous day. Someone had said, 'Put three young saplings in the same hole and they'll grow together as one.' I had no idea whether the practice was sound but the metaphor had pleased me nonetheless. As I threw the earth onto the thick young tangle of roots, I felt as though I was committing our love to the ground by this simple ceremonial act, so that we would grow together, straight and true. Strange that, for I'm not known for acts of sentiment. The third sapling was the house, of course, binding us ever closer together.

And then it began again. It started with the builder's tools: a drill lying on the floor suddenly starting up and spinning around in circles; then the CD player flaring up into life at full volume. And strangest of all, my engagement ring vanished for over a week and suddenly reappeared one morning in the bathroom sink.

Peter got the brunt of it. Again, the hand on his shoulder pushing him hard down the spiral staircase as he was showing a group of American visitors round the house. He was lucky to escape with only minor bruising to his arms and legs that time. I wasn't imagining it (how many times would I say that in the coming months!), there was a subtle shift in the atmosphere of the house – an edge, you might say. And neither of us could bring ourselves to speak of it; to speak would be to imbue the shadows with life. The growing weight of evidence mustered in the wings, like the seventh wave before it breaks itself upon the shore.

We'd both started working again. We needed the money. It would go towards the restoration of the gatehouse. Work had begun on it in earnest and it was already gobbling up all the money we could shovel into it, like some roaring red-hot furnace. I'd set up a bindery – in a room they had called Sir Richard Wynn's Chamber in the seventeenth century. A tiny oak door in a wall of panelling led into it and a second door up three steps led out of it. It suited my needs perfectly. Here I could bind my books in relative seclusion, while Peter spent his days report-writing in another lonely corner of the house. The bare stone walls were fire-scarred and the ceiling sagged like a taut bladder when it rained, but I'd managed to achieve the look I always hanker after – that of the alchemist's laboratory. There were rows of thin-necked phials on shelves, crusty cauldrons of glue and, of course, my favourite emblem: an hourglass on a wall bracket. The implements of my trade have not changed much since the medieval period; the bone folders, the bodkins, the sewing frames are all the same. I was working on my largest commission yet: twenty-seven volumes of Dickens, to be bound as a run in red morocco with decorated spines. Hang the expense, my client had declared. It was the best kind of commission.

There in my sequestered, sunless cell I worked alone day after day. I began to know the books intimately. Their soft, tobacco-rich, pre-war smell; the steady, solid weight of them in my hands and the pulpy, satisfying thickness of each page. The laborious process of rebinding each one was under way. I stripped the volumes of their damaged outer cases and gave each book new cream endpapers. I rounded and backed the spines to revive their original shape and then lined them with mull and brown paper. I lavished particular attention on *Great Expectations* – Miss Havisham was a favourite heroine of mine. Fifty-two newly cut boards lay waiting to become the hard covers of each book. I had a stack of twenty-seven rectangles of red leather to pare for each spine. This is an involved process whereby the suede underside of the leather is gradually stroked away by the use of a spokeshave and sharp knife to make the leather malleable. Pared too thinly and the leather looses its tensile strength; too thickly and the leather proves unworkable. A consistent smoothness has to be maintained throughout, otherwise the divots and bumps show on the finished binding. Leather is expensive: one slip of the knife and the whole piece could be ruined.

It is during moments like these, when I am most absorbed in my paring, that I first become aware of a presence in the room. A presence somewhere behind me, faint, clouded; gone the instant I turn around. I peer into the empty, dust-moted gloom: nothing, except again that shift in temperature that makes me gather my cardigan tighter about my shoulders. It happens again the following day, like the eyes of some Jacobean portrait burning into me; but there is no portrait, just an empty wall pockmarked with damp. I feel a cold shiver slide down my back but I am curiously unafraid.

Any number of ghosts were supposed to haunt the house. Was it the servant girl who was cruelly murdered and walled up by Sir John Wynn? Or was it Sir John Wynn himself, who'd been seen so many times around the house in his tall black hat and ruff, melting into walls where once there were doorways. Instinct said not. I couldn't quite put my finger on it then, except that the presence I felt exercised none of the customary reserve of your average spook. Whatever it was, it wanted to make itself known to me.

Day after day I sense the waiting, watching presence lurking in the shadows. I try to concentrate on my work, paring away at my pieces of leather with a rhythmic rowing motion of the arms, watching the crumbling shavings rise like little waves from the throat of my spokeshave before disintegrating into dust. Each day I allow the presence to linger a little longer behind my back before I spin around, and each day I am offered a small gift of information. Is someone playing games with me? Did I catch a scent of musk or cloves or some such spicy perfume? Next, I'm sure I catch a flash of blue silk, like a strip of sky, out of the corner of my eye. And once as I walk into the room, I hear a burr of laughter.

This is how it is meant to be. It is a woman who shares the same dead air as I. I am caught on her spool, her inexorable spool, as she winds me into the penumbra of her world. I see her in my head as clear as day: sallow-faced, dark-eyed, a little smile curling about her plump lips, and the blue dress she wears edging the whiteness of her *décolletage*. I know her name is Margaret. But there's something else too. What's this? She's angry with Peter. Call it what you will – feminine intuition, cerebral osmosis – I have this knowledge at my fingertips: I just know.

My bindery is suddenly the coldest room in the house. I work on my books in wraps. Small udders of glue encrust themselves on my mittens. My feet are so swollen with chilblains that they no longer fit in my shoes. For relief, I drag my toes across the coconut matting we have laid in our bedroom. They burn pleasantly and then seeringly as the blood rushes back into them.

I try to find a way to make my head overrule my heart. I spell out the essence of the thing to myself. Hard-headed reasoning – that's what's called for. So, a woman appears to me almost every day in my bindery. Tell that to the judge and they'd send round the men in white coats. But it's true. To be specific: I don't actually see her as a solid apparition; it's more I have a sense of her – I see her clearly in my mind. The icy timbre of her voice caresses my temples with spite. I know she has a high forehead and brown ringlets that fall luxuriously against her cheeks. Her eyes are close set and her nose is pinched and a little too prominent to qualify for archetypal beauty. With stealth, she crawls into the moon-plagued regions of my mind. She comes when I'm least expecting her, when the brain is disengaged and I'm absorbed in some automatic movement of the hands. I begin to await her presence with the hard-edged cravings of an addict. I guard my secret jealously.

I know I'm changing. Peter tells me so. He says, 'What's happening to you?' And he hangs his head like some dejected puppy. And this is the part that's hard to dredge up: she wants desperately to come between us. She's all mischief and sharp keys. For the first time in seven years, discord seeps between us. We jar. We argue. I'm cold and implacable. A void has come between us and I can't cross the gulf. She bars the way and she won't let me back to him. It makes me wretched but I just haven't the strength to challenge such a menacing force.

Once, when I am alone in the house, I hear footsteps outside my bindery door. I call out. Silence. Strange, though all nine doors into the house are open, the castle's gates are barred and bolted. It would be hard for anyone to pierce the membrane of my seclusion. I go out and follow the click-clack on the boards. Upstairs now, on the top floor of the Solar Tower. I run up the spiral staircase feeling the cold twist of stone beneath my fingers – the room is empty; downstairs in the Great Chamber – empty. I hear a door bang. It's not the wind – there is only one door in the house the wind can open and it's not that door. I go down into the Lower Hall – it is hollow in its emptiness. I must see whether there are any cars parked in the lay-by. I try the door but find it bolted on the inside. I try a second door, but it too is bolted. I run round all nine doors in the house, the very doors I have opened with my own hands not an hour ago, and find them all bolted on the inside. Someone or something has locked itself inside the house with me. I dig deep inside myself and like a pea in an empty barrel I dredge up my last grain of courage. It propels me forward through the house; my body is as rigid as a board.

Of course, there is no one, not a whisper, not a sigh to flutter the cobwebs. It's just another of her games. There's a bird, a wren, I think, trapped in the Great Chamber. It keeps banging itself relentlessly against a window pane and the moment I move closer to open the casement, it suffers a crouching, paroxysm of fear and then begins to beat its breast even harder against the brutish glass until there's blood from somewhere, streaking the leaded panes. Tears start in my eyes. I leave it to its martyrdom and rush around blindly unbolting the doors, attempting to defy the supernatural with a blanket sweep of cold rationale. I have never felt so alone in all my life. If I am the bird, then my brown-eyed girl is the cat that waits insouciantly to pounce.

I've reached a point where an enigma will not suffice. I want answers. I need reasons why our lives have been turned upside down by a pale voice from the past. I visit a friend who I know to have carried out extensive research into the paranormal.

'Voices in the head, you say?' I nod (I've gone beyond the point of bashfulness). 'Hmm. Could be any number of things. Prenuptial nerves, for example. Or it could just be a simple case of possession.'

'There's nothing simple about this case of possession,' I snap.

He ignores my comment and continues, 'I believe it is possible for the organic and inorganic material core of a house, ie the wood and, particularly, the stone to absorb a strong charge of emitted emotion. In effect, the matrix of a wall can act like a sort of crystal set; it's the same principle, after all. You may be sensing the reverberations of an energy still locked in the walls from an incident which took place hundreds of years ago. You've just tuned in to the right radio station, so to speak.'

It made a kind of sense. Her malignant frequency was rife on the air, like the sound of an organ resonating in the aisle of a church. Echoes. I was picking up the echoes of her sadness. And of her anger.

Coincidentally, around this time, a medium calls at the castle. She says she was just passing the gate and felt an urge to come in. Ironically, I'm instinctively suspicious of someone who claims to have a taproot into the super-natural. She must be in her seventies at least. She has red hair coiled up in a bun and bright green, owl-like eyes magnified behind thick spectacles. Unsubtle use of the eyebrow pencil makes her look in shock. In another age, they'd have dunked her in the river for a witch. There are all kinds of chains and beads hanging around her neck. Against my better judgement, I unchain the gate and let her in. Immediately she has entered, she stops. Her smile of introduction drops from her mouth and the roses in her cheeks recede like dipped headlights. Her eyes are fixed on some distant place that is not within my range of seeing.

'No, I'm sorry, I can't enter,' she's saying. 'I can't enter, there's something here. There's a wall. It won't let me in.' She backs towards the gate and once outside shakes her head as though she's trying to dislodge a stuck bone in her psyche. If she's a fraud, then the performance is chillingly convincing.

'My dear, there are problems here. Let me help. I can exorcise the pain,' she says as she reaches out and takes my hand. 'Let me exorcise the pain.' But I'm unsettled by that word exorcism. When we first moved in, Peter and I vowed we would never exorcise the house. We felt the historical layering of events and personalities was integral to the character of an ancient house. To tinker with the delicate equilibrium was to undermine the indefinable, like an overzealous archaeological dig: the earth never went back the same way. In our experience houses became sterile, literally spiritless places, once they'd had their memories wiped clean. Nothing would ever inspire us to whitewash

Gwydir's past. The atmosphere was like a well-ripened Stilton, a palimpsest of richly textured historical odours.

Still holding my hand, the woman stared into my face. Did she see the real meaning in my eyes? It would take more than a few cheap spells and the swing of an incense burner to banish Margaret from my life. She dwelt in me now as wilfully as she dwelt in the house. I shook off the medium's hand, a little harder than I meant to, and a look of comprehension passed over her face, like a child who has suddenly discovered the answer to a riddle.

In another prism of our lives, the gatehouse progressed at draught-horse pace. There were complications; there always are when there isn't enough money to make the problems seem irrelevant. The roof was seemingly held together with hairpins and there was nothing for it but to take the whole lid off and start again. At some point in its life, Arthur Clegg had turned the gatehouse into an office. It was where he kept his money hidden. At the end of a good day on the gate, he'd squirrel away bundles of fivers into some kind of home-made safe and when he was counting his money no one was allowed to enter.

It was a tiny little building, just two rooms deep, but with a bit of imagination we felt we could rustle up a rentable cottage out of it. Attaining a regular source of income was forefront in our minds: if we tackled the gatehouse first and then moved on to the coach house, in time we would have two cottages bringing in an income which would help fund the more muscular renovations on the castle itself. That, in any case, was the plan. The gatehouse was originally part of a larger range of buildings which had more or less been swept away in the early nineteenth century, the gatehouse itself having been reduced at that time to a single storey. Sir John Wynn's study had occupied the lost upper floor. It was here in the 1780s that the manuscript of the *History of the Gwydir Family*, written by Sir John, was found among the rat droppings and corn chaff. This document told us so much about life at Gwydir in the 1580s. A note of Sir John's wardrobe, for example, was contained within it, taken on the eleventh day of June 1616: 'one tawnie klothe cloake, lined thoroughe with blacke velvett . . . two blacke velvett jerkins . . . one suite of blacke satten cutt . . . nine blacke felte hattes, wherof fowre bee mens hattes . . . one guilte rapier and dagger, and one ridinge sworde with a scarfe, with velvett scabbards'.

Now the gatehouse was another little mongrel of a building, uglified in 1950s Hansel-and-Gretel-style, and in desperate need of beautification.

Jim Busby was not the obvious choice of craftsman for the job, but he was our only choice. Will had gone AWOL about three weeks ago and hadn't been seen since. It was no good pleading with him. We knew from experience he'd be back in his own good time.

'Trust me,' Jim said in his South Walian singalong voice, 'it's aw right, roofs are simple.' Peter employed the sceptical use of the raised eyebrow and remained silent. There was excitement when we found a loose slab in the floor just in front of the fireplace. The slab was lifted to reveal a sort of foyer into a larger cavity, which had obviously served as

Arthur Clegg's makeshift safe. Who would dare to put their arm in first and what would we find – Mrs Clegg's jewels or one month's forgotten takings? Peter was coerced into plunging his hand into the dark hole. He kept the suspense hovering for moment after tense moment as his hand searched the blackness. But the joke was on us, for there was nothing save the ubiquitous Coke can ring-pull.

One morning, Jim came back from feeding his goats in Blaenau Ffestiniog with the news that he'd found us a roof for the gatehouse, which was ours for nothing, provided we collected it by the end of the afternoon. It was the timber from the roof of a big, old derelict hotel, on the high street in Blaenau Ffestiniog, which was about to be renovated with European money and turned into flats for the homeless of Birmingham.

Collection was down to us. Jim leaned back against the kitchen sink, lit himself a cigarette and ran his fingers over his unshaven chin as though he was looking for something he'd put down ages ago. The collection bit had stumped us.

'It'll have to be the Land-Rover,' he said gravely.

'No, not the Land-Rover,' said Peter. 'Out of the question. It's got no tax or MOT and the brakes are dodgy.'

The Land-Rover was a family heirloom. It was a big, old, army, long-based thing with a canvas top that we couldn't bring ourselves to scrap. Occasionally we used it to collect logs from the forest, but that involved dirt tracks not official, law-abiding tarmac. I groaned out loud at the prospect of a group activity. I wasn't in the mood for company at all. I resented anything that took me away from the bindery and the thought that I might miss a rendezvous with my dark-spirited *alter ego*. The presence in the bindery had moved into a new phase of disquiet. There was a feeling of crescendo in the air. I craved her company more than ever now.

A yawning chasm was expanding daily between Peter and me. Her whole *raison d'être* seemed to be to make his life as miserable as possible. The previous day, he'd taken me by the shoulders and with tears in his eyes he'd said, 'I can't take much more of this. It's the house, isn't it? It's too much. It's come between us. Let's sell it, if it would make things right between us again, the way they were.'

In reply, I'd said: 'The wedding's off,' and walked out of the room, careful not to slam the door behind me. But something had pulled at my heart. This monster I'd become wasn't me at all. The trouble was I couldn't resist her commands. She was a greater force than our earthly bonds could vanquish. Or was she?

'We'll take the Land-Rover,' I said. Anything to disagree with him. We went on the back roads. I drove, Peter fumed.

I read somewhere that Blaenau Ffestiniog has one of the highest levels of rainfall in the British Isles. Dark, brooding, wet – quintessentially Welsh and enigmatic. The mist was hanging low over the bracken-scented hills as we began our steep descent into the town, past the slate mines where thousands of men had toiled beneath the ground in caverns, chipping and digging their way to the earth's core. The slag heaps were like burnished canyons of graphite, as though a million pencil tips pierced the earth's crust. Slate from Blaenau Ffestiniog had roofed every corner of the world, at one point or another. Like coals from Newcastle and sand from the Sahara, slate was Blaenau's synonym. Its other export was Ivor the Engine.

It was a poor place now; the industry had dried up long ago and the slag heaps were just reminders of its arduous past. The hotel on the high street was boarded up. The roof had come in at the back after a snowfall and the timbers were strewn about like a giant game of straw sticks, picked up and dropped at random.

We filled up the Land-Rover with timber until its canvas sides heaved like a trawler's fishing net. Never in my life had I broken the law before.

'Put more in,' I said. 'Fill it up.' The tyres sagged; the Land-Rover was overfilled and I knew my car insurance did not cover me to drive it. I smiled. Beaming with the exaltation of it. Margaret was with me. It was the first time I'd felt her presence outside the bindery. Peter sat and stared miserably out of the passenger window.

'If someone's going to lose their licence, let it be me,' he'd said, but I'd paid no attention. Jim sat like some gnomish referee between us, his knee getting in the way of the gear stick. The Land-Rover was heavy to drive with the extra weight. We flew back down the hill towards Dolwyddelan, canvas belts flapping, pieces of wood slipping.

'For God's sake, slow down, will you?' said Peter. But I was having fun. I pumped the brakes with all my might and tried to hold the steering wheel steady when we rounded a corner. Twice the back end swerved out of control and I clipped the verge, and twice I just managed to pull it back onto the straight.

But disaster did not strike that day, though when we arrived back at the castle it felt as though I'd used up one of my lives and stolen a life each from Peter and Jim. I could hardly stand for trembling. Peter was white with fury, but he didn't say a word. He just walked away into the garden as a man walks into the sea; and later, from the bindery window, I saw him leaning with his head against the silver trunk of the copper beech.

No, disaster did not strike that day. It struck the following afternoon instead. The three of us were working on the gatehouse roof. It was wet and cold and the predominant colour of everything was grey. Even the trees, particularly the trees and the land, were close to seeming drained of colour. There had been a vague plan that we'd all pitch in and strip the roof. We'd kicked around all morning, listlessly brewing up cups of tea, putting off the moment when we would push ourselves out into the rain.

Finally, the clouds parted. The flat roof, part slated, part felted, was just strong enough to take our weight. Jim directed the proceedings from the parapet, with his long nose stuck in a mug of coffee. We hacked and beat a hole through the felt, scooping it up with sharp spades, and then prised up the rotten sheets of ply. Within an hour we'd made a sizeable hole in the roof, but there was one last very stubborn piece of ply which just wouldn't budge, no matter how hard we tried to persuade it.

'Peter,' I said, 'go down beneath and whack it loose from

below.' My orders were becoming more and more imperious, uncaring to the point of forgetfulness. Margaret was with me every waking moment now. And in dreams, too. I'd listen to her filling me up with spite: like two young witches we cooked up a malicious cauldron of wrath, and I was absolutely certain now that she was not merely the spawn of my imagination – how else did I know so much about her? She'd found a willing host in me. So Peter went below and whacked the roof with a long iron bar, while I sat on top hanging onto the rafters. And unbeknownst to me, the glinting, steel-tipped spade bounced towards the hole behind my back, towards a resolution of sorts, towards the thin-boned skull of my beloved.

Strange the way accidents always happen in slow motion. The world stopped spinning for me at that moment, the birds stopped singing as the spade made its slow, purposeful journey towards the edge of the hole.

You get a good view of the castle from the top of the gatehouse roof. I remember seeing some plant life clinging to the interstices of a chimney stack and thinking how we ought to get up there and remove it when the weather improved. I had time to think all sorts of things. I caught sight of the spade about two hops from the edge and still my hands didn't fly to its splintered hilt. I just watched it happen like some gormless puppet whose master, on a whim, refuses to work the strings. She played the final card with that spade. It was like being revived from a dead faint with iced water. Oh, my God. I shuddered out of her embrace. But not in time. Not in time.

The spade sliced and it cut.

They say, *amor vincit omnia*, love conquers all. I held Peter's hand as they wheeled him into the X-ray room, a sick feeling bubbling in the pit of my stomach. He lifted his head and said, 'I know who she is.'

I mouthed, 'I love you,' and his head fell back against the pillow. I'd told him everything on the way to the hospital, sobbing and tripping over my words: I told him everything I knew about the woman who had haunted me and hated him. I described her eyes and the pattern of lace on her cuffs and the tiny mole she had on her lower right-hand cheek, while he held a towel to his head and the blood erupted in little geezers, spotting the white with red so that the towel became like snow after the fox has made its kill. It felt as though some great bird was rising from the surface of my conscience. In sharing my secret, her power was diminishing.

The spade had sliced and it had cut – falling sharp edge down straight onto Peter's head. It had knocked him sideways onto the floor. I slid blindly through the hole in the roof and was by his side in seconds, sitting amidst the fallen timber and discarded roofing felt, cradling his head in my lap. The gash followed the line of his parting. The birds had begun to sing again. I could hear blackbirds and rooks, and the sound of a whining chainsaw echoing down the valley.

The doctor pulled the curtains back and said, 'Lucky he's tall. Had he been a foot shorter it might have killed him. Just the ten stitches and concussion. Mind you bring him back immediately if he complains of headaches or dizziness.'

I caught a glimpse of my face in the ward mirror; my cheeks were streaked with dirt and tears. Our clothes were filthy from the roofing tar. But Peter with his bandaged head was smiling. For the first time in almost two months we were both smiling and holding hands, and the old love we'd shared for the past seven years was enfolding us again like the bliss of a fur-lined coat on a snowy day.

'I know who she is,' he repeated, once we were back in the kitchen, and this time I incredulously absorbed the meaning of his words. 'Your description – there's only one person it can be. Her name was Lady Margaret Cave.'

The one detail I'd omitted to tell him in my description of her was that I knew her name was Margaret. I shivered and took a gulp of wine. He kissed the top of my head and left the room, then returned with a book. It was a copy of the *Calendar of the Wynn Papers* – the collated collection of manuscripts relating to the family.

Lady Margaret Cave was the daughter of Lady Eleanor and Sir Thomas Cave of Stanor, Northamptonshire. Sir John Wynn, the first baronet's eldest son, had married her in 1606, and she had brought with her a dowry of three thousand pounds – a sizeable fortune for the time. The marriage had started well enough. He said she had 'a gentle good soul . . . was sensible and willing to please'. She became pregnant the following year and Sir John eagerly anticipated the birth of a son and heir. But by the close of that year something had happened between them. Whether it was a consequence of the birth of her first child is not known, but Sir John's opinion of her had radically altered.

In a letter to Margaret's mother, Sir John Wynn senior complained that Margaret's 'disposition and imperfections caused his son to appear as a man dead or forlorn', and that her state of health had ruined the marriage, which had been in his view 'an unlucky match and one which threatened to overthrow his house and fortunes'. She was a dissatisfied and bitter woman who quarrelled with the servants and generally made life a torment for her husband. Sir John exercised his fatherly authority by making his son 'unwillingly stay with his wife to see whether it be possible to make him love her'. The experiment failed and, to escape her, Sir John embarked on a European tour. It was to be the final act of separation in what otherwise had been a loveless marriage. The young Sir John never returned to Gwydir. In 1614 in the Italian city of Lucca, he died of the plague, aged thirty-one.

I felt stunned. Though I'd never heard or read of this woman before now, I knew it was my Margaret the letters described. She was still exercising her dissatisfaction with life four hundred years on, trapped in some dreadful loop of time, and like a wolf which clings to the back of a lamb, she had attached herself to me. The anger and the loathing she had felt towards Sir John had been transferred through me to Peter. He was the focus of her pent-up negativity. And now it was over, as swiftly as it had begun.

In discovering the sad facts of her life, we had unwittingly created the mechanism for her final release. It wouldn't be an honest end if I said I hadn't felt her absence wistfully in the beginning. To have another live inside your skin, who then departs as breath on glass, does not take place without some sense of loss, some sense of a small death having taken place inside.

The postscript to this tale occurred just recently when we found a nineteenth-century account of Gwydir, giving the names of many of the rooms. My bindery was mentioned, the room where all this had happened: 'Sir Richard Wynn's Chamber', it said, 'also called the Ghost Room'.

10
A Notable Wedding

$\mathcal{W}$as that it? Had the house finally accepted us? An eye for an eye; a possession for a possession, so to speak. One thing we never joked about was Margaret. It was done, it was over, no need to revisit that particular skeleton. A calmness settled over everything like dust. And summer was suddenly upon us. The wisteria dripped its mauve blooms down the front of the house like scented wax. The swallows were back in the porch. The horse chestnuts turned out in full regalia. Sheep streamed through wooden gates like spilt cream on to the rich river pasture, where the swans sometimes came up to graze. Those naked, frigid winter days had lengthened almost imperceptibly into tall, graceful days of a rich consistency. It was like coming out into the light after a long spell in a darkened room. For the first time since moving in, I divested myself of a thermal layer. Losing a skin was liberating. I felt light and perforated as though the weather fell through me, not against me in the manner of a buffeted pier.

The bats, too, came out of hibernation. They were alarmingly like those fake ones you can buy in joke shops at Halloween: big and black with rubbery arms and ears like daggers, with not a hint of a smile on their snub-nosed faces. In winter they lived inertly in the dark recesses of the priest hole and garderobe tower, hanging upside down like used tea bags pinned to the ceiling. The summer air coaxed them out of their torpor as the voice of a loved one calls a patient from a coma.

I'm not fond of things that flap in confined spaces. All's well in the right place, but having to cross the Hall of

Meredith at night to reach the bedroom, with a swarm of bats swooping about, sent the mildest *frisson* of panic down my spine. Some evenings, if the bats were feeling particularly sociable, I would cross the hall swinging a tennis racket about my head to ensure they kept a respectful distance away from my hair. Whatever anyone tells you to the contrary, a bat's radar system is not infallible. I have had some pretty close shaves in my time, when I've actually felt their wings brush against my face like an eyelash kiss. Looking up into the upturned hull of the hall roof from a position of safety was to see them weave a figure of eight into the ether; over and over their habitual criss-crossings scored a path in the air and each morning the velvet cloth that covered the table in the Hall of Meredith was littered with the carapaces of dead insects.

A seasonal migration of sorts was also taking place among the day-tripping fraternity. The lanes, now ripe with cow parsley, were filling up with small ladies in large cars – who wore headscarves and had trouble reversing. Coaches began to slow down outside the gates so that passengers could watch the peacocks displaying their tail feathers on the roof of the gatehouse that overlooked the road. It was a sure sign that people were on the move. Slowly, and to our infinite surprise, the bell began to ring, and it felt a little like a harvest festival after the lean pickings of a particularly hard winter.

What did the visiting public make of Gwydir? Were our visitors charmed by the shambolic nature of the place? Did they warm to the sight of a marauding peacock taking a short cut through the house from one part of the garden to another; or the biscuit-tin lid that covered a hole in the floor of the Great Chamber? Did they understand the flaking paint aesthetic or the reason why we chose not to remove all the cobwebs from the rooms? If pushed to manufacture a statistic, I would say that some people got it and some people didn't – about seventy-thirty in our favour.

There was a good deal of scope for the unforeseen error: such as the time, one afternoon, when Madoc deposited the contents of our laundry basket around the house, while we were out buying doors from an architectural salvage yard. We came back to find a trail of silk underwear (dating back to when I could afford such things) scattered at intervals across the floorboards. A little lace-trimmed something here, a little embroidered number there, strewn carelessly upon the stairs. Our highly skilled team of personnel had failed to check the house before allowing people in. I gathered up the trail of smalls like Hansel and Gretel in the forest and eventually the crumbs led me to two sniggering schoolboys and their red-faced father. My arms overflowing with laundry, I smiled sweetly and tried to look insouciant. 'Everything all right?' I asked.

'Splendid, thank you,' stammered the father. 'But could you tell me, is the house still lived in?'

I just couldn't bring myself to claim responsibility, so I said: 'Yes, a young couple have bought it. But I'm afraid they're away at the moment.'

It was a far cry from the slick image of the National Trust: the overpriced tea; the pot-pourri-smelling gift shop, the hard sell on membership, etc. Our visitors didn't get any of that here, that was for sure. No, we prided ourselves on offering an experience that was altogether different from the National Trust.

They got a house that was still moving with the tide – clink of chisels echoing round the courtyard; the odd mouse's kidney deposited under a table by one of the cats; Peter's handwritten signs on chairs that said things like: 'Touch me not, for I have not thy youth'. There were no ropes or headphone tours, or ladies with badges on their lapels dropping suggestive hints about the fifth baronet's sexual proclivities. There was just Sven, Will, the Busbys and, if absolutely pushed to it, Peter or I. The trickle of people who visited the house did not warrant the employment of a full-time gatekeeper. Whoever was closest to the door answered it when it rang. When it did ring, everybody ran in the opposite direction. Only the really persistent were granted access. And the one thing that really persistent people love to do is talk. Now I know my limitations. I know I could never be a nurse, a cook or a submariner; I know that I can't make a white sauce, climb scaffolding or run up a pair of curtains. I also know that I am pathologically incapable of engaging in casual chitchat. I see it as an omission in my social make-up, a personality defect, which has undoubtedly led to a number of missed opportunities in my life. My presence would have sounded the death knell across any self-respecting tea table in an eighteenth-century salon. I can no more talk about the weather than I can talk about rocket science, and I think I can speak fairly authoritatively for Peter on this point, too. We both loathed the kind of impromptu garrulity one was forced into when the bell rang. Perhaps therein lay the seed of our attraction for one another. I would rather go to the bottle bank or clean out the cellars than answer the door.

A faint ripple of unease – no, a veritable choppiness – therefore clouded the waters of our inadvertent descent into the public service industry; an industry which ultimately depended upon our ability to make people feel welcome and at ease. There was even loose talk going about that we might do bed and breakfast once the roof of the west wing was back on and perhaps even weddings when the gardens were more respectable. This was hostile territory for two, young, burgeoning misanthropes who valued their privacy above all else. But Dame Fate had this habit of leading us down improbable culs-de-sac and there was no use railing against it; you just had to relax and, as they say, go with it.

When cabin fever impinged we would go for long, memorable walks up into the hinterland of hills, where bracken covered the seam between valley top and rocky escarpment. Following a cobbled Roman road one day, we ate our lunch in a chambered cairn and later looked over a derelict shepherd's cottage, still with its rusted old kettle upon the range, as though it had been left too long on the heat and had boiled the whole cottage dry. The dogs lapped from a rusted bath full of water. The track led on across the hills from one Roman camp to another and it was as though we were walking on the spine of a prehistoric monster. The heat of the afternoon beat down on our backs until we came to a stone circle where sixteen stones lay half buried in the stiff grass. And inside the circle, as though under the power of a spell, we lay down and fell asleep with the skylarks nattering overhead. It was the first, proper, dreamless sleep I'd had since Margaret left. It was a healing sleep. I slept until a hovering bird of prey covered the sun and I felt the shadow of its wings fall across my face.

'Ladies, gentlemen and dogs,' announced the Reverend R. Mortimer to the assembled congregation, 'it gives me great pleasure to welcome you all here on the occasion of this happy union . . . '

Gwydir's little chapel up on the hill was a vision of pastoral simplicity – a quote from Hardy, perhaps – in its cool, garlanded beauty. I remembered to take a good look around me as we stepped over the threshold: at the flowers entwined around the gallery balustrade, at the painted angels up on the ceiling and the edifying black-letter text which never failed to move me, 'Watch! For you know not ye day or howre.' The bell in the chapel bellcote was tolling and the harmonium piped up the Old 100th. Such a sound! To me, so evocative of country churches and clean-shaven young men marching off to war. The door to the chapel was open wide. The drone of the organ floated out and mingled with the pale scent of the fir trees, and the swallows flew in and out, banking hard against the canted ceiling, fanning the cheeks of the angels with their wings.

'The Lord ye know is God indeed,' boomed out the congregation, who were in fine voice that afternoon. Sir Richard Wynn, the fourth baronet, who became chamberlain to Queen Catherine of Braganza, built this chapel in 1673, a year before his early death from the plague. It was sequestered up here on the hill among the holly trees, a place for private prayer and contemplation. The marriage ceremony that was taking place, our marriage ceremony, in fact, was the first proper service to be held here since 1921.

In keeping with tradition I had kept everyone waiting a good twenty minutes while the zip of my dress decided not to zip up. This dress, which was made by a friend of mine out of some cream damask curtain material, was as itchy as a sack. The Lady of Shallot would have sold her soul for this dress – it was right off her coat hanger: tight bodice; buttons from bosom to floor; very full in the skirt. I even got to wear a discreet chatelaine around my waist and a plaited gold band around my head. But at the moment when minutes began to matter, the dress decided not to zip up. My mother, with her knee in the small of my back, took matters into her own hands and forced the zip, which promptly tore away from the dress material. It was out with the needle and thread. Peter's mother held the fabric together while my mother stitched away. And there was a strange symmetry to this little ceremony as though, unwittingly, we were enacting some ancient, pagan custom. My mother, in a tizz by now, stabbed me while she stitched all the way up my back, so that the fabric of my dress was stained with little beads of blood which resembled a stitched wound, with the zip running up the middle.

Finally, I'm in. We're done. I had hoped to walk up to the chapel but was advised that mud and cream damask were cat and dog when it came to compatibility. Beneath the trees, where the sun had failed to reach, the ground was still touched with summer dampness.

There were two bags of sand on the back seat of the car. No matter; I drove myself up to the chapel and there was Peter by the door, looking tall and serious in a dark morning suit, saying, 'Come on, come on,' as the bell-ringer stretched his tolling to a fifth round. My bridesmaid, Carw, scrambled over the bags of sand and out of the back of the car. Entwined in her collar was a garland of pink dog roses. I realised I'd left my prayer book and posy on the kitchen table.

'Give me a second, will you?' I found a nice patch of leggy daisies which I rustled up into a chain for Carw to wear around her neck, while I purloined her roses for my posy. We were ready. I could hear the congregation rising noisily to its feet, the organ wheezing into tune. I was thin on fathers at the time, so Peter took my hand and we walked together up the short aisle. Humidity speckled the flagstones. A candle guttered on the altar. The ceremony began. I saw the wet lips of the old Welsh preacher murmur the immortal words and, with the swallows larking above our heads, we repeated after him the sealing promise of our futures together. Carw lay down on the train of my dress, adopting that classic lurcher pose where nose follows the streamlined finish of outstretched legs. Madoc had been excluded from his duty as page because Carw was in season and this was very definitely not the occasion for monkey business in the aisle. My mother was getting emotional in the front row. I could almost hear her say that favourite phrase of hers: 'Darling, my cup runneth over,' in a theatrical bass. I found myself thinking of those three yew trees we had planted in the same hole and how they had survived the worst of the winter floods and frost and were now thriving in spite of the vicissitudes of nature. I caught a flash of the scar the shovel had made on Peter's head, as he slipped the ring over my finger. None of our friends and family who were present (dappled now, in their pews, by the window light as the sun shifted lately across the sky) were aware of the blizzard we had come through to reach this place of ineffable contentment. What had happened with Margaret seemed beyond expression: then and now it was a blur, fading fast into hindsight and the dim ether of our collective remembrance.

'You may kiss the bride,' said the reverend. And the bell began to toll again and everyone was on their feet, and the blizzard now was a blizzard of scented rose petals raining down in a shower of crimson light.

There was music and dancing later that night. Since we were so concerned about the look of the whole proceedings, we asked our friends to arrive in black tie to avoid ambiguity on the dress front. Thus, the smell of mothballs drowned out the smell of my cloved oranges.

We cut the cake with a long rapier that had, by the look of it, seen some pretty serious action in its day. The relief of having got the formalities over with was immense. The chandeliers blazed, the gardens were alight with flaming torches. We'd found two musicians from Bethesda who came in medieval costume and cranked out the rawest-sounding Elizabethan jigs I'd ever heard on rude crumhorns and bloated sackbuts. But it worked. It was a sound that Gwydir purred to. We danced by firelight and though you're not supposed to enjoy your own parties, we did wholeheartedly. The evening span on and Sven got tipsy on the fruit punch.

Later, much later, when everyone had retired to their respective tents and hotels for the night, Peter and I found ourselves alone in our makeshift bedroom where every expense had been spared. A honeymoon was out of the question in our straitened circumstances. Our bed of bubble wrap had progressed to a proper mattress on the floor, but our clothes still hung from broom handles across the windows, fulfilling the dual role of wardrobe and curtains. The windows were open and the scent of the honeysuckle around the terrace arch wafted up on the night air. The garden was as still as I'd ever known it, just the cry of an occasional peacock breaking the silence. Dawn was starting to break over Town Hill; it was hardly worth going to bed.

And so, in the pale light of the candlelit room, I handed Peter a pair of scissors and with infinite care he began to cut me out of my dress.

11
Lost Treasure

*N*ot long after our wedding we had a visit from Bob Llysafon, our neighbour, who farmed the land adjacent to us. His real name was Bob Owen, but in Wales farmers are often known by the names of their farms, rather than their surnames, a tradition which may perhaps be a hangover from the days of land feuds.

He was built like a jockey: short and wiry, with a sharp, elfin face. There was something of the leprechaun about Bob Owen. He was either to be seen elevated above the hedges in the cab of an old horse wagon or else scraping the tarmac in a bright red sports car. His father had bought the land that surrounded the gardens of Gwydir when the estate was sold in 1921.

A waft of Imperial Leather greeted me as I walked into the kitchen. Bob and Peter were discoursing on the whereabouts of Dafydd ap Siencyn's cave, which was said to be somewhere high up in the cliffs above Gwydir. The (not very serious) hope was that the cave might still contain the plundered treasure Dafydd stole from the rich to give to – himself. No one had found the cave in living memory and that was an irresistible cause for action as far as Peter was concerned. He was planning a sortie sometime soon.

'Now, that's not why I've come,' interrupted Bob. 'I've come because of this,' he said, nodding and tapping his pocket. 'I've got something here you might be interested in.' We were agog with anticipation but tried our best to sound disinterested in case he was about to try to sell us something.

'My father came to the sale here in 1921. I've kept this

all these years. Thought you'd be interested to see it.' He reached into his pocket and pulled out a rolled-up tube of paper. It smelt of tobacco and elastic bands. He dragged a chair across the flagstones and threw himself down onto it. I flinched as the joints cracked under his weight but he was too caught up with the unfurling of the document to worry. I, too, forgot the chair when I saw what it was he was smoothing out on the table. There, among the crumbed remnants of our hurried breakfast, was a copy of the original sale catalogue from 1921: to us a rare and hitherto unglimpsed paper grail which our swelling archive of Gwydir-related material sorely lacked. It had a faded green cover with a picture of the castle on the front, a Gwydir in its heyday sort of photograph, or the kind of image you might once have seen on a tea towel.

I turned over the first page: 'Gwydir Castle, Caernarvonshire', the heading proclaimed, 'the Ancestral Home of the Ancient Wynn Family. The illustrated catalogue of the valuable contents of this important and historic mansion embraces a very rare and valuable collection of fine 16th to 18th century furniture.' It felt like a piece of the jigsaw had slotted comfortably into place – an awkward piece of sky, say, or an enabling bit of sea. Feverishly, we turned over the pages; it was sumptuously illustrated with sepia photographs of the most delectable oak furniture.

'Look at this,' said Bob, pointing to his father's spidery handwriting in the margin: 'One thousand guineas for a table! Have you any idea what that would buy you in 1921? Probably three Rolls-Royces, or a small estate in Berkshire, I shouldn't wonder.'

'But that's not just any old table,' murmured Peter 'that table was made for Sir John Wynn in 1596. Look,' he said, pointing to a squiggle on one of the legs, 'there's the crest of the Wynn family: the eagle and the lion.' On the next page there was a picture of an old oak cupboard, the doors of which were heavily carved with heraldic devices. 'Just listen to the catalogue description,' said Peter, his excitement swelling like a soufflé. 'The renowned John Wynn Court Cupboard carried out in fine proportions in Gothic design and surmounted by a canopy dais, having been made in 1535 for the one whose name it bears.' There again, carved in relief, was the eagle of Owain Gwynedd, the fleur-de-lis of Collwyn ap Tangno, the lion of King Cynan, all proudly proclaiming a family lineage which stemmed from the belly of the Welsh princes. These pieces had in all likelihood been made from oak that had grown in the Gwydir forests.

The sale had evidently caused quite a stir. Ward, Price & Co, a firm of Scarborough auctioneers, were 'honoured' to handle the sale – on whose behalf, the catalogue omitted to say. But we knew from other sources that the Earl of Carrington had owned the house around this time. A marquee was erected on the lower lawn and the furniture was hauled out of the castle for perhaps the first time in three hundred years. There were over eight hundred lots in all, encompassing everything from an antique mahogany bidet to the 'Panelled Tudor Mansion House' itself.

But the biggest surprise was yet to come. We turned over a foxed page. Momentary confusion overcame us as we tried to make sense of what we were seeing. Here, before us on the page, were ghosts of another kind. There were pictures of two rooms within the house as they had looked in 1921. Surely some mistake had been made in the cataloguing of these pictures? These shadowy interiors, sumptuously panelled, were more reminiscent of the grandest of houses: a Blenheim or a Chatsworth, even. But no mistake, the captions confirmed that Lot 65, 'The remarkably fine Tudor linenfold panelling to the Oak Parlour' and Lot 88, 'The remarkably fine 17th century panelling to the Dining Room', were indeed Gwydir's own. We stared at the page, caught up in the thrill and the sadness of seeing Gwydir's past at once twinkle and then recede as we remembered that these rooms no longer existed. In our minds we overlaid the images with the reality of the rooms as they looked now, and it was hard to equate the bruised walls and charred beam ends with the rich riot of carving that bolstered the walls in the catalogue.

But what was this? We read on. Both rooms were being offered up for sale in their entirety: the panelling, the doorcases, fireplaces – even the ceiling beams were available for purchase if the price was right. A groan of exasperation broke from Peter.

'The vandals,' he said simply and quietly, and I felt, in this instance, I couldn't better that, so I sat staring at the faintly misted interiors, shaking my head with doleful incomprehension. The images were mesmerising. It was like meeting a famous relation you never knew you had.

Lot 65, the Oak Parlour, was the first room to be auctioned. Though the walls were robed in the most exquisite linenfold panelling, the fireplace attracted the attention like a bursting comet in a dark, moonless sky. It was outrageously ornate. It bore the date 1597 and in the centre was the Wynn coat of arms swamped by a swirl of ornament. Flanking the arms were large figures of Julius and Augustus Caesar in full armour. They bore the startled expressions of real people who had been told to stand very still in a niche, on pain of a gruesome death. Light fell in through the windows and illuminated the family motto: '*Nec Timet Nec Tumet*' – 'No Fear, No Vanity'.

Lot 88, or the Dining Room, was a little younger than the Oak Parlour. It was mid-seventeenth century and more refined in its way, more sophisticated. There were two photographs of it in the catalogue, one of the doorcase and one of the fireplace. The photographer had homed in on the show-stoppers. The doorway was like a portal to some other world, with carved and twisted columns holding up an elaborate cornice which bore a frieze of grapes and lions' heads. In all it was almost twelve feet high. There was a similar hallucinogenic quality to the fireplace. Again, two twisted columns entwined with vine leaves and grapes supported the overmantel, which bore the Wynn coat of arms in the centre. The whole thing was a fuzz of carved decoration. It was like falling headlong into a very sophisticated doodle where the virtuosity of the carver left you groping for superlatives. The catalogue even went so far as to suggest that the room had been designed by none other than Inigo Jones, architect to the court of Charles I and the 'father of English Palladianism'.

But what had happened to these glorious interiors? Had

both these rooms been dismantled and taken from the house at the sale in 1921, or had both remained and burnt in the fire of 1922? There was a cryptic little message at the bottom of both descriptions that said: 'This lot may be withdrawn if sold with the property as it stands, or if the property is unsold.' Somewhat annoyingly, Bob's father had omitted to record the price of either Lot 65 or Lot 88; we wondered why.

'I'll leave it with you, then,' said Bob, breaking our reverie. 'But look after it, that's a family heirloom that is.'

Something in the back of my mind was trying to make itself known. Something June or possibly the jester had said all those months ago . . . 'whole rooms taken to America'. Then, it had seemed like another tall story of the ship's timbers and secret passage variety. Now, suddenly, it didn't seem so tall at all.

The long summer shadows began to lengthen. The days were now blissfully warm, hot even, and we'd slip into the pale evenings: a bottle of chardonnay chilling in the fountain among the iris, our hair furred with dust and hands stinging from lime, but so happy, so memorably happy it frightened me. We sipped and we dozed on the parched grass while the nuthatches hammered at the bark of the cedar trees and the peacocks came out like rainbows all over the garden. I thought, it's not right to be this happy, something will happen to take it all away from us, I must not give in to hedonism – that's a convent education for you. And Goethe's words resounded in my head: 'Nothing is so hard to bear than a train of happy days.'

But I did allow the happiness to swell up between my

toes and fingers, and the trespasses and the hurts of a lifetime began to fall away from me, and I felt myself growing and expanding daily in the cloistered sanctuary of the garden. We'd come through the worst the house could offer and now it seemed to be taking us to its heart. It's amazing what high, protecting walls can do for those of a sensitive disposition. I began to feel secure. God knows, there was little enough to make us feel secure: each day we braced ourselves for the next crisis. Opening the doors to the public was a little like crouching behind a sandbag, having pulled the pin from a hand grenade.

There had been two close shaves in the space of a week. An elderly couple with two impish little grandsons had paid their dues in expectation of an energy-expending hour in the adventure playground we didn't have. The usual spiel was administered at the door: no touching, no sitting, go wherever you like but do not open a closed door – I liked that Bluebeard touch. But when those chocolate-covered grandsons discovered there was no adventure playground to wreak havoc upon in the grounds, they turned their attention to the house instead. The four-poster bed, with its fine cut-silk coverlet and hangings we'd just fashioned *à la* Knole's Spangled Bedroom, became a substitute bouncy castle. The Lower Hall became a bowling alley as they sent our collection of cannonballs clattering across the flagstones; fragile chairs were climbed upon; the Grappolini twins ran for their lives. And while the children rampaged, the grandparents rummaged in coffers and opened closed doors. Granted, there is something totally irresistible about a private sign on a door. I've done my fair share of peeking along with everyone else. But this small family went beyond the bounds of mere curiosity: they penetrated the inner sanctum – they got themselves into our bedroom! And there I found them, browsing idly through the books on the oil drum that served as my bedside table, the children helping themselves to Peter's stash of Strepsils, the grandmother redoing her lipstick in my mirror. It was a scene strangely reminiscent of Goldilocks but without the charm or porridge. Suffice it to say, things got off on the wrong foot with this family. Warmed-up words were exchanged and positions defended ('but the door wasn't locked', from the grandmother; 'what else would you like, the shirt off my back?' from Peter) and everyone was left feeling a little harried, a little frayed at the edges.

I managed to eject the children into the garden: fewer things to break in the garden. The peacocks had taken to the trees and were honking and hooting at the indignity of having their tails stamped on. I was skirting the walls like a sniper, trying to keep the boys in my sights until I lost them momentarily behind a hedge. And then just as the grandparents homed into view, there came the most almighty yelp. I broke cover and emerged just in time to see Carw sink her teeth into the vealish behind of a small boy. It was all over in seconds. The dogs had been sunning themselves in a secluded spot behind the hedge when the boys had set upon them with sticks – no self-respecting lurcher would take that sort of behaviour on the chin.

Visions of lawsuits and ruination flashed before my eyes. I saw the nip of reality, inflate to the size of a savage attack in the law courts. I recalled the cheque for public liability cover still awaiting postage on the kitchen table. Just as the implications of this omission were registering in my mind, the grandmother, who was by this time on her knees consoling the screaming child, suddenly said, 'Be quiet. Look over there.' She pointed to a place beneath one of the cedar trees and said, 'Can't you see her?' We all squinted into the distance. There was nothing except a cloud of midges hanging in a pool of golden light. The garden had become very still. 'There's a woman in a blue dress looking at me over there.' In spite of myself and all I was feeling I felt a smile drift across my face. I was sure it must be Margaret; but Margaret on a mercy mission this time. Margaret trying to make up for all the hurt she'd caused. 'Darren, shut up. I've just seen a ghost,' yelled the woman at the small boy. I could have fallen to my knees in gratitude. The dog bite was superceded in importance by the woman's vision. The child could see there was no more mileage to be had out of screaming and so lost interest in the whole affair and wandered off to look for something feeble to torture.

'Didn't you see her, didn't you see her?' the woman kept asking. But nobody had, and that only worked to exacerbate her unease yet further.

'Would anyone like some tea?' I ventured nervously – for it still could have gone either way.

Silence from both of them and then, 'What a grand idea, luv,' from the husband. I suppose, historically, tea has always been a great averter of disasters. It's like the barking dog who suddenly lies down and allows you to tickle its tummy. No offence meant, eh? None taken.

And so there we can leave the little gathering enjoying their tea in the late afternoon sunshine of the courtyard, while we pluck out another scene at random from our lives at Gwydir. The two small children, for example, I found setting light to one another with candles in the Hall of Meredith. Or rather the brother, who was seeing how fast his tiny sister would go up in flames. My fault for leaving a lighted candle on the table, you might think. They'd cycled up from Llanrwst still in their pyjamas and stockinged feet – there is that kind of Dickensian aspect to certain quarters of Llanrwst. Somehow they'd got themselves into the house and up the spiral staircase. I enter stage left to find sister suspended above lighted candle by brother – nice and inflammable those pyjamas, the sleeve is catching on a treat. There's something rather eerie about these two, they don't say a word. And the sister has an absolutely blank expression on her face; it is beyond resignation. I pluck her up and douse her under the cold tap for a good minute or two. Her sleeve is smoke blackened and shredded at the cuff, but miraculously her arm is unharmed. I set her down at the wicket gate and they both run off to their bikes which lie in a discarded tangle on the gravel beside the holly tree. They pedal off furiously but the little girl looks back at me, risking a wobble, before flashing me another penetrating non-look.

Peter has his own stories to tell. When we meet up in the evenings we spill them out on the table, like coins from a cloth bag. His quota for the day includes a delightful Muslim family who come in with prayer mats rolled up under their arms. Having picnicked among a stand of nettles in the Commemorative Garden, they gather in the courtyard for prayers. A new sundial has been bought for the column which sits in the centre of the knot garden. It hasn't yet been fixed and it affords Peter much pleasure to spin it every so often and then watch the men in the party try to check their watches by it.

The Muslim family look at the sundial to get a compass fix and then . . . what's this? . . . all eight of them promptly kneel down on prayer mats, with their rears facing Mecca. Is this not a terrible slight against Allah – will this bring the walls of Gwydir tumbling down – should Peter tell them and thus interrupt their prayers? Too late, the time lapse of indecision voids all quandary. Prayers are quick today and Allah is forgiving. They wave their goodbyes and thanks across the courtyard and the incident is soon supplanted by a visit from a family of American Wynns, who are paying their biennial homage to the old homestead. Our household scatters at the prospect, but Peter is caught in the butterfly net of forced amiability and spends the next two hours discussing the quarterings of Bradley Wynn, Junior the Third's family tree.

Our days were peppered with interactions such as these. People wandering in, asking where the cash dispenser is or whether we serve cream teas, or did special rates for pensioners. We began to learn a few old naval tricks: such as if you wanted to cross the house without getting stopped, you cloaked yourself with the mantle of the tourist by putting on a coat and popping a guidebook under your arm. Our visitors' book soon began to swell with messages of good will: 'Thank you for saving our ancestral home,' written by a Wynn, for example. And, to our delight and astonishment, suddenly our coffers did not ring entirely hollow. At the end of each week, having turned out our pockets and metaphorically (and sometimes literally) searched down the sides of chairs, we always had just enough to pay the builders.

Two of the worst chimneys were completed. Will was painfully slow. He'd start at one o'clock, have three mugs of tea and tell you exactly how he intended to tackle the chimney: how many bags of lime he'd need, how many bags of sand. And then he'd clock off at four, saying he had to go and feed his sheep. But sometimes he'd fix up spotlights or stay up on the scaffolding until eleven at night. He was a bachelor. He kept strange hours.

Most days you'd hear the words 'Hold it', as the builders waited for a visitor to pass beneath a dangling piece of coping stone. The roof was almost back on the west wing. The soft, comforting thud of lead being beaten into the parapet gutters echoed round the courtyard and was accompanied by the straining whine of a drill raking out the cement-pointing between each stone. Syd and the Scouse Git toiled languorously. It was hot and shirts were justifiably removed, much to our annoyance. At five, they'd go off to our local waterfall, the Grey Mare's Tail, and take a shower. At five we regained the blissful silence of the house.

No need to improve on the imagery of the Grey Mare's Tail. Suffice it to say, the cascade of water fell from a high point to a low point in a secluded little dell not far from the castle, like a grey mare's tail. The spray from it was bracing even in summer. It had the feel of water that lived most of its life under ground.

When Sir John Wynn was laying out his new garden at Gwydir in the 1590s he was quick to realise the potential of the Grey Mare's Tail. He took a spur of water off the cascade just before it tumbled down the incline, and then channelled the water along a leat which ran across the hillside above the castle. The water collected in a header tank and the pressure was enough to feed a fountain in the gardens. Sir John loved tampering with watercourses. He'd already made the River Conwy navigable up as far as Llanrwst, so that select household supplies could be barged up from the walled town of Conwy: hence the need for a causeway at the bottom of the garden. The iron rings for tethering boats are still there in the stomachs of the oak trees that grow on the riverbank. Sir John shipped his wine, his tobacco, and even his funerary monument up from London in a boat called the *Hopewell*.

We had an ancient right to the water that fed the fountain and one of our projects was to get it going again. The Victorians had 'rusticated' the fountain basin by dumping a couple of tons of quartz crystal in it. But if you looked closely you could just see the octagonal-cut stone-surround of the early basin. In the centre was more quartz out of which the jet of water was supposed to issue. Nothing had issued for years. Water seeped from somewhere into the basin, but mostly it was full of yellow flag iris and congealed frogspawn.

Firstly, the leat that crossed the fields needed digging

out. There were horses in the fields: three picturesque old nags that had been spared the cat-food tin through the intercession of a kindly old farmer. But they'd trampled down the banks of the leat over the years and the water now escaped down the slope of the field. The plan was to redirect it back along the leat and into the slate tank. The leat was over three-quarters of a mile long. We spent three days digging it out. And when we had exhausted ourselves, Sven took over. On one day he came back with a buzzard with a broken wing. He'd seen it fly into a telegraph wire and had watched it fall like a rock to the ground. I can see him now standing in the moody light of the courtyard, wearing his Umbro T-shirt, clutching this haughty, scowling bird, which seemed contemptuous of the rest of us but strangely not of Sven. Anyone could see that there was mutual respect between them. He gave it to the local buzzard man to repair, and later we heard that the bird had made a full recovery and had been released with a swoop back into the wild.

The leat was now clear and ready to accept water. There had been a minor glitch where the water crossed under the road, but nothing that a good rodding couldn't sort out. The flow of water was regulated at the waterfall by nothing more technical than a rusted sheet of corrugated iron with bent-up sides. The simpler the technology, the less room for disaster. And, make no mistake, there was plenty of room for disaster: such as the eighty-foot drop to the right that you had to negotiate while crossing the treacherous, algae-slicked rocks to reach the iron sheet. With one arm thrown out like a trapeze artist, Peter deftly heaved the sheet into place and the water began to course into the leat. It was a deeply satisfying moment; by the end of the afternoon the tank had filled up. By evening there was still nothing issuing from the nozzle of the fountain.

'The pipe's blocked,' said Jim.

Jerry said, 'I knew it would be,' and suddenly I wasn't at all sorry that he was leaving on the 8.15 from Llandudno Junction the following morning. As a working holiday, it had not been without its ups and downs. He'd tried to turn us into squaddies, to his sergeant, and we were having none of it.

Jim had the idea of blasting out the pipe with a CO_2 canister. There were a couple of them lying hazardously around in the shed, left over from June's *beer-cellar* days. The nozzle itself was buried in the island of quartz in the centre of the fountain. You had to walk a plank to reach it across the moat of sludge and frogspawn. I volunteered Jerry for the job. I knew he would go on a point of honour.

'Of course I'll go,' said Jerry. 'Give me the canister.'

He edged his way across the plank. The iris stems wound round his legs like a knot of affectionate cats. With his weight bearing down on it, the plank brushed the surface of the sludge. We watched from the bank, with arms folded, waiting to see what would happen when the plank snapped. The plank didn't snap. Jerry smiled smugly back at us when he reached the island and then began fiddling with the nozzle of the fountain.

'Good Lord, it's a toad!' he shouted. 'There's a toad wedged in the pipe.' With pinched fingers he plucked the putrefying corpse from the end of the pipe and, as he did so, a plume of black sludge erupted like a geezer straight into his face. Now, I've never found slapstick comedy in the slightest bit funny but this was a vintage performance. Everyone, bar Jerry, found it hilarious. There he sat, looking like the victim of a robbery, while the pipe cleared its throat of sludge into his face and all down the front of his shirt, until at last the flow ran clear with mountain water. To his infinite credit (given the hysteria that was emanating from the opposite bank) not only did he take the whole episode with good grace but he also got the fountain going. I felt a pang of affection for him. Once the nozzle was screwed back into place – no small feat given the pressure – the water issued forth in an elegant, twenty-foot spout. The jet rose up in a column of pearly light, as though the quartz crystal was throwing pieces of itself up into the sky. And in the house that night we fell asleep to the sound of tiny stars falling into teacups and it gave one a glowing feeling to wonder when that sound had last echoed round the Dutch Garden.

Peter loved the idea of the rigid stateliness of Gwydir's early gardens. Quoting Alexander Pope, he would mutter about the 'princely mockery of formal gardens'. I knew what he meant. In the late sixteenth century you could have cut yourself on the topiaried hedges that edged the paths. The Renaissance garden was an allegory for life. It was an attempt to recreate divine harmony as expressed through symmetry and perspective, it aspired to recreate the Garden of Eden before the Fall. The making of a garden was an intellectual pursuit and, in keeping with his time, Sir John Wynn loved formality. His bards wrote poems, or cywyddau, as they're called in Welsh, extolling the virtues of the gardens. There were quinces, oranges and lemons, topiaried figures, tunnel arbours and endless paths. And of the maze in the garden, Siôn Tudor wrote: '*Laborinthws dlws, duleision – didlawd/ O waith Ded'lws dirion*' ('A fair labyrinth, green and fecund/ The work of gentle Daedalus').

Granted, the Victorians, or whoever it was, were naughty to have overlaid much of this, but I found the remnants deeply mysterious. There was the promise of something more beneath the surface, like the city spire of some lost civilisation protruding through a jungle tangle. And as the days grew hotter and the ground became more and more parched, a small, slow miracle began to take place before our very eyes. The lost civilisation of Sir John's day began to lift up through the grass. The ancient paths and terraces were suddenly there for all to see in the sandpaper surface of the baked lawns.

You got a birds-eye view of the garden if you climbed out of the top-floor window of the Solar Tower onto the new lead roof. Believe me, it was worth tenderising your feet on the boiling leads for a glimpse of Gwydir as it had looked *circa* 1600. The yew avenue was suddenly a homage to formality. Four huge whale humps closest to the house denoted terraces leading down to the fountain, and beyond an axial path had scorched the grass with smaller radiating paths leading off between the yew trees. Lumps and bumps had appeared and only to be guessed at foundations – of what? Perhaps the bard's 'cabins, brightly built', or his 'castles of wood', or his 'fair towers set in pearl . . . a paradise in which to rest', or 'a picture of Troy on a regal lawn'. These poems and the risen shapes in the grass had given us a blueprint for the future restoration of the garden.

But I knew I'd mourn if we lost the romance of the garden altogether with too much clipping and snipping, too much pleached choreography. The garden needed to feel the wind through its hair; it needed to have the freedom to unlace itself from the whale-boned restrictions of rigid symmetry, if it pleased.

A fair bit of chaffing occurred on this point between Peter's desire for formality and my love of free-flow romance. Not much, but enough to leave a mild inflammation in the air whenever it was mentioned. I felt there was a compromise to be had. He was welcome to his pleached limes, if I could have my orchard, underplanted with wild flowers. He could have as many raised parterres and busts of Apollo as he wanted, as long as my roses would be allowed to spill out onto the paths.

But how easy it was to run on with our plans beneath a freakishly hot, late September sun. I was all for biting off more than I could chew, but even I was ever mindful of the floods which lurked slyly behind the month of November. Before any restoration of the garden could take place, the flooding would have to be addressed. And given that our immediate concern was to make the house wind and watertight before the coming winter, building dam walls around the ten-acre perimeter of the garden was not a top priority.

One thing I would say about gardening was that I didn't

like doing it. I liked the planning bit and the end result, but I didn't like the mechanical heave-ho bit in between. Same applies with food: I love eating but I don't like cooking. What I knew about gardening would fit on the head of a pin. Ask me to distinguish a rose from a tulip and I'm on fairly firm ground. The rest is as dark an alchemic secret as turning base metal into gold. Peter was the same. He could talk professorially about the Mannerist gardens of Salomon de Caus or Pliny's influence on the rise of the Humanist garden, but ask him to prick out ten seedlings and he was dead in the water. And here we were, suddenly responsible for a north-facing, frequently flooded, Grade I-listed garden. It was like being at the wheel of a Formula One racing car without quite knowing where to put the key.

12

American Connections

$\mathcal{W}$e tried to keep our minds on the multiple jobs in hand, but the notion that those two panelled rooms might exist somewhere kept popping up like a bunny at a shooting range. We were forever wandering back to the catalogue in the hope of wringing a clue out of it. And clues did come, eventually, after a bit of teasing out. We telephoned the auctioneers, Ward, Price & Co of Scarborough – not Ward, Price & Co any more, as it turned out, but some rather blander name like Smith Brown Estate Agents.

'Pity you didn't call last month,' said the woman on the the phone. 'You've just missed Mr Price.'

'When will he be back?' I asked. 'I'll call later.'

'No, I mean he passed away last month. But he was the one you needed to talk to. He was a young porter at the time of the sale and later became a senior partner in the firm. We were clearing out his desk only last week. Funny you should call now. There were lots of papers relating to your place. Was quite the sale of the century, wasn't it?'

'Papers, you say? I don't suppose it would be possible . . . ?'

'I'm afraid we incinerated them all, just last week. Well, they were so old, you see. Fire hazard when you have limited office space, as we do. But old Mr Price had talked about your sale in the past. Some famous American had turned up and bid for a couple of lots. Caused quite a stir, apparently. Oh, what was his name? You know, he was in that film *Citizen Kane*.'

'Orson Welles?' I suggested incredulously.

'No, not Orson Welles. He played the character. Let's see. Oh, what was his name? He was very rich; had the affair with Marion Davies, sold newspapers. Yes, that's it: Hearst – it was William Randolph Hearst. Mr Price often talked about him. A tricky chap to do business with, apparently.'

Now this was a turn-up. I'd seen *Citizen Kane* once, years ago, but I hadn't forgotten it. I hadn't forgotten the snow-shaker scene at the beginning and the sleigh, 'Rosebud', the mysterious focus of the film. And Hearst portrayed brilliantly by Orson Welles as the grand, mercurial newspaper tycoon – more money than sense, as my mother would say. It was difficult to connect the glitz, the spin and the razzmatazz of '20's America with Gwydir. What had Hearst been chasing at the sale and why? We pursued the enigma round and round like a pea on a plate that wouldn't be caught.

We'd made a pact, you see. When Bob had left us poring over the catalogue that morning, we'd said to each other that whatever happened we owed it to the house to try to find the missing lots: not every single teaspoon, of course – let's be realistic. Just the important pieces; the furniture that had been made for the house, for example, and the panelling from the two rooms if, that is, it hadn't remained in the house and been burnt, as appeared to have been the case. We owed it to the house to at least find out what had happened to its illustrious contents.

Hearst now gave us an important lead. Given that all the documentation relating to the sale had been destroyed just the week before, he was, in fact, our only lead. So we began to pursue him, really for the sake of not knowing what else to do. I got a biography of him out of the library. A big biography of the kind that is awkward to read in bed. And gradually I synthesised the facts of his life through the incident and reported anecdote in newspaper clippings, letters and the often poisonous remembrances of close friends. The details of his life are well known. For our purposes, however, it was enough to know that he made a vast fortune selling newspapers, and, as a footnote, we have Hearst to thank for the advent of tabloid journalism. His was no ordinary fortune though; this was a fortune that made him one of the richest men in the world and, correspondingly, he lived a life in which tinfoil stars rained down perpetually upon his head and Hollywood draped itself around his neck like a fake fur. But in the end, for all the glitz and the glamour, he comes across as a tormented character driven by an insatiable desire for power, which led his biographer to conclude that 'he was a man more great than good'.

So into our lives stepped William Randolph Hearst. It was what he did with his money that interested us. At the time of our sale Hearst was spending, on average, $1 million a year on antiques and works of art. He was no connoisseur; any man who could dress in noisy, plaid sports jackets and Hawaiian shirts could be no *aficionado* of art. You got the feeling he might just as well have been collecting toby jugs or chamber pots, but his budget allowed for something more, something beyond the baroque imaginings of the most irresponsible of Renaissance princes. He relied on an assortment of dealers to furnish him with the best European splendours money could buy. 'You want a Spanish cloister, sir? Then you shall have one,' said his agents, and a Spanish cloister was found, demolished and duly shipped to California, every one of its 36,000 stones carefully packed in straw in 10,700 crates.

His mother said that whenever her son felt badly he would just go out and buy something. It must have been that Hearst felt badly most of the time, given his appetite for stockpiling priceless treasures.

But his greatest folly was yet to come. The mule train of crates full of European booty were wending their way to San Simeon, the castle he was building on a hilltop in northern California. It was Hearst's most lavish creation: born out of fantasy and obsession, and butter-patted into shape by the architect Julia Morgan, a small, old-fashioned woman who wore horn-rimmed spectacles and Queen Mary hats. In the film they named it Xanadu and a stately pleasure dome it most definitely was. In real life it was called Hearst Castle – though it was not so much a castle but more a palace, in *faux* Spanish style. It was vast, it was kitsch and it never would be finished. In the end, it bankrupted him.

So this was a start. There was a whiff of an answer here. Hearst was buying at our sale to deck out the halls of San Simeon with Gwydir's fixtures and fittings, that much seemed certain. It was an attempt to bestow upon the new the kudos of the old; it was a validation of sorts.

The Getty Museum in Los Angeles held the Hearst archive. It took no time to wing off a letter to the archivist to see whether any mention of Gwydir came up in their records in relation to Hearst. And then there was nothing more to be done except to wait and speculate further as to where Gwydir's lost treasure might now be residing.

By the time autumn began to crisp the edges of the valley, the trail had certainly picked up apace. We were several letters down the line before we received our first really big bit of news. The first letter came as a response to our letter to the Getty Museum, informing us that William Randolph Hearst had indeed made acquisitions from the sale at Gwydir. Information was sketchy, they told us, as the pieces were no longer at San Simeon, if they had resided there at all, but they understood that something from Gwydir Castle had been bequeathed to the Metropolitan Museum of Art, in New York, by the Hearst Foundation in 1956. This was our first major breakthrough. They gave us a contact address and we lost no time in writing to the Metropolitan asking for further information.

A reply on heavily embossed paper arrived. It smelt costly. It came from a Mr William Weaver, an associate curator of the museum, who politely informed us that yes, indeed, they were in possession of an item from Gwydir Castle which had been purchased by Hearst from the sale of 1921 and had later been bequeathed to the Metropolitan Museum. Peter read out the letter, his voice taut with nervous anticipation. The item in question was listed as Lot 88 in the original sale catalogue, namely the seventeenth-century panelled Dining Room. It consisted of the oak wainscot panelling itself, an elaborately carved baroque fireplace and doorcase, and a leather frieze designed to run between the ceiling and the top of the wall panelling, presumably also of seventeenth-century origin. It was presently being stored in a warehouse in New York and, as far as he knew, it hadn't been out of its original packing crates in its entire seventy-five-year exile.

Now this metaphorically sent the champagne corks popping. Hardly able to believe what we were reading, we scanned the letter again just to be sure. Gwydir seemed to be saying, 'Good, now it's time for me to reveal a little more of myself to you.' There was no doubt in our minds that a big, big personality, with a director's hat on, sat behind the damp lichen-covered façade, working the controlling arm of its own destiny – and ours for that matter.

This room of old Gwydir was at least safe, then. It hadn't been burnt or chopped up for kindling or joked up by Arthur Clegg. The knowledge that it survived somewhere intact and unharmed gave me a feeling akin to having won a mighty victory against some ruthless property developer. Something of beauty, almost as precious as a green field or an oak tree, had been saved from destruction, for had it stayed in the house it would surely have burnt in the fire of 1922. The hero of the day was, of course, Hearst – an unlikely saint given his predilection for European plunder. Nevertheless, by default, he had saved our room from destruction. He once, apparently, chopped the legs off some extremely rare late medieval chairs because they wouldn't fit under a table. He might easily have done something equally horrific to our room: fitted out his steam room with the panelling, for example, or made place mats out of the leather frieze; but the fact that the crates had not been opened since 1921 boded well for the condition of the room.

Naturally, the next step was to ask the Metropolitan Museum whether it would ever consider repatriating the room to its rightful home. It was a long shot, given that museums rarely release treasures held in trust for the nation, but what was the harm in asking we persuaded ourselves.

We'd co-opted the use of a fax machine in the stationer's shop in Llanrwst to speed up the sluggish business of transatlantic correspondence. When a message arrived the shop staff would telephone us and we would rush down the causeway with the dogs, along the riverbank where the tidemark of last season's flood still remained high in the hedgerows. A few intrepid dragonflies flitted over the surface of the water and the cattle dallied in the shallows, swinging their tails over their backs at nothing in particular. We would cross Sir Richard's fine old bridge into the town; the same Sir Richard whose room we now pursued in America. How he'd chuckle. On the pavement, outside the shop, we read the silky-paged messages.

The response to our request was formal and to the point: de-accessioning of works of art was often a contentious issue and was a matter for discussion among the trustees of the museum. William Weaver would put our request to them and would report back in due course. In the meantime he felt it would be beneficial to meet, preferably at Gwydir, so that he could vouch for the authenticity of our request before it went in front of the trustees.

Now this was a turn-up. What was Mr William Weaver

of the Metropolitan Museum of Art going to make of 'Crotchet Castle' with its bats and its steel props holding up the ceilings? And more worryingly, what impression was he going to take back with him to the trustees. He knew nothing of our circumstances. All he'd had from us were a few heavily edited letters in which we spoke rather grandly about the 'phased programme of restoration' we were currently undertaking at the castle.

An image of him began to form in my mind. The eggbox-thick writing paper had done it. I saw a tall, rather reserved man: studious, patrician, clean-shaven. And there was no escaping it. Given that we lived on part of the map that said 'here be dragons', we felt bound to issue an invitation of dinner and a bed for the night, not imagining – for a moment – that he would accept. But he telephoned the next day and said 'only too deli'did', in his cool, Bostonian drawl.

I now knew how Lord Leicester had felt when he heard that Queen Elizabeth was pencilled in for a stopover at Kenilworth Castle during one of her legendary progresses. A kind of panic gripped us because Gwydir had such a lot to lose if it didn't go well and we weren't even properly habitable yet. We were still in our underclothes as far as respectability went. The camp beds and candles were a novelty to our friends who could later go home to their inexhaustible supply of hot water and towelling bathrobes, but Mr William Weaver of the Metropolitan Museum might not so easily fall for Gwydir's rustic charm.

There was nothing for it but to put him in one of our so-called display rooms. The Royal Bedroom was where the

Duke and Duchess of York, later King George V and Queen Mary, had stayed in 1899, and it was also the room where Peter had first felt the hand on his shoulder pushing him forward towards the fireplace. Spartan would be a luxurious description of it. No heating or electricity, of course, just rough rubble walls and bare boards patched over with bits of old biscuit-tin lid, and windows that blew out a candle straight away if you held it up to the stringy bits of lead which were doing their best to hold the square panes in place. But to give it its due, it was very atmospheric. It was effectively an upstairs parlour where you might have eaten a mutton chop in the old days, with a little four-poster bed in the corner. It was sparsely furnished on account of the fact that we'd run out of furniture. A couple of tall, William and Mary, cane-backed chairs were propped against the walls. There was an oak coffer at the foot of the bed and a little gate-legged table with some lilies in an earthenware jug, and a single bell candlestick. We fleshed it out with a few leather-bound books and the odd bit of red velvet, and by the time we'd finished it really did resemble an interior in a Dutch old master.

'Please, just call me Bill,' said Mr William Weaver as he banged his head on the gate. He was immaculate in his pale grey suit, the lick of a pink handkerchief protruding from his lapel pocket, hair faintly greying at the edges of his pale scholarly face. Just the right amount of expensive cologne breezed in with the smell of quality leather luggage. An icy wind laden with drizzle whipped up the corners of his jacket and he flinched because it felt like some mischievous imp had applied a cold spoon to his back. I knew that feeling well, but I now took precautions – in the form of thermal underwear well tucked into thick woollen tights.

'Look! It's a wonderful day for rainbows,' I said, trying to take his mind off the cold. Up there, with the sunburst, was an immaculate rainbow, a cliché of a rainbow in fact, with its slim bands of ultra colour spanning the house like a halo. I said a silent thank you to God for putting on such a good spread for us just when we needed it, because it was obvious Bill was impressed. So impressed that he didn't look where he was going and stepped into the biggest pile of peacock guano you have ever seen. Peter silently directed him to a patch of rough grass where he endeavoured to remove the vile-smelling substance from the stitching of his fine Italian shoes.

We went inside and it was straight to business. First, he wanted to know which part of the house the panelled room had come out of. He unclipped his briefcase, started taking notes. We took him to the wing June had vacated not twelve months since. It was still virtually as we had found it: patio doors and rotting pink bathrooms; even the urinals, I was ashamed to notice, were still there. He raised an eyebrow. I closed the door quickly.

'Is this your handiwork?' he asked, gesturing upwards towards a singularly nasty swirling plaster ceiling.

'Oh no,' we gasped, horrified that he thought we could have been capable of such a travesty of style, such an ugly disfigurement. Though this wing was a victim of the '60s, it had been further embellished in the mid-1980s by June and company. The work looked newish even now, ten years on.

'No, we had absolutely nothing at all to do with it,' said Peter decisively. 'If you were to give us the room back, this would all have to come out. And it wouldn't break our hearts to see it go, I can tell you.'

Bill said very little on his tour of the house. We had tried our best to exclude the doves from the Great Chamber but they had found new and ingenious ways of breaking back in. He eyed them on the lintels with deep suspicion. He said even less when we showed him to his room. In fact, his silence was beginning to make me sound like some garrulous old hen fresh off a nest of eggs. Thank heavens we'd had the foresight to ship in reinforcements for supper, in the shape of two hearty friends not known for the subtle use of the pause when in conversation. Lucy was a vague acquaintance of Bill's from the museum world, and Michael was an old friend whose sound judgement in all matters temporal had frequently bailed us out of trouble. Both were the epitome of respectability. And the good thing was you could just press play, sit back and happily enjoy an evening's entertainment with these two.

I don't mean to be unkind to Bill. He was perfectly sociable. Who knows, we might even have found each other at a party under different circumstances. But there was no avoiding the fact that he was here to vet us, and we were cripplingly aware of the telescopic range of his assessor's eye spooling in great knotty bits of information about the house and us to take back to the trustees.

'We'll be dining in the Hall of Meredith this evening,' I said at his door in my finest Nancy Astor voice, 'do join us for a drink at eight.' Little did he know we had never had a grown-up dinner in the Hall of Meredith before. Little did he know our friend Michael had had to bring the cutlery and plates with him because we didn't have enough to go round. What we forgot (how *could* we forget?) was that a room as big as the Hall of Meredith was virtually impossible to heat, with no source of warmth except for an open fire. There was no insulation in the roof – just the sky and then stars. And the fireplace, though spectacular, would accept a forest or nothing. Still, it might have been cold, but only the hardest heart could fail to have been moved by the sight of the hall by candlelight. In relation to the vastness of the rest of the room, we sat like five peas huddled round a spinach-leaf table in front of a mediocre fire. I suppose only Peter and I would have called it mediocre, but that was because we had become fire snobs. It had to be a perfect triangle of orange flame with a blue heart to be considered a good fire by us. And we had now refined the art of fire-lighting to just half a bar of firelighter – no mean feat if the kindling was damp.

When the wine was being poured, Bill covered the top of the glass with his hand. 'I don't drink,' he said gloomily. Now this was a blow. All hope of salvaging the occasion was dashed on the rocks of his abstention. For one thing, it might have brought a little colour to his cheeks, warmed him up even. I doubted his thin jacket could be keeping out much of the cold. Not a drop passed his lips the whole evening, but plenty passed our lips, and Michael's tongue got looser and looser as if he was taking it out for a walk on a long piece of string. Everyone was having a roaringly good time by the pudding stage except Bill, seemingly, whose torso was as straight as if it were strapped to the ladder-backed chair he was sitting upon.

And then suddenly Michael was off on a joke. Oh, no! The table fell silent as the joke began to slip off the rails, plunging headlong into an embankment of risqué innuendo.

'. . . He said I meant a hookah not a hooker,' screamed Michael. 'D'you get it?'

'Yes Michael, we get it,' said Peter, suddenly sober. Michael was splitting his sides over the joke but nobody else round the table was laughing, least of all Bill.

Peter cut in and said, 'And now I think it's time for bed.'

Bill got stiffly to his feet, moving as one who had spent the last two hours stuck on a meat hook in a butcher's refrigerator.

'Perhaps tomorrow before I leave we could talk about the room,' he said coldly. 'Good night, everyone.'

'Night, night,' said Michael, still wiping the tears from his cheeks. 'Sleep tight, mind the bugs . . .'

'Michael, it's time for bed,' said Peter.

The following morning Bill picked his way stiffly down the spiral staircase. He made no attempt to hide the fact that he had three shirts on underneath his jacket.

'I've always wondered what sleeping in a Dutch painting would be like and now I know,' he said, with the hint of a smile on his face. He left Gwydir in a hurry, waving away breakfast, mumbling something about trains and planes, promising he'd be in touch – in a way that made us think we'd never hear from him again. We hadn't even talked about the room.

We knew we'd blown it. We felt utterly despondent after he left, as though we'd somehow let the house down. Much later, Lucy told us that the story of Bill's stay at Gwydir was spreading round the museum circuit like a bush fire. He'd said it was the coldest night of his life.

Meanwhile, the gap in the centre of the house continued to throb as an amputated limb is said to throb long after the surgeon has cast it away.

13
Strange Bedfellows

$\mathcal{S}$trange how sitting in a different part of a house can give you an altogether different perspective on life. I'm out on the lead roof overlooking the whole garden and very lovely it is too, with all the trees for miles around in full leaf. Our valley is very green indeed. That is the one compensation for having so much rain. I expect there are others, but they haven't come to me yet. It's that time of year, just before the farmers cut the silage and the fields are the most luscious colour – the kind of green that looks as though it has been artificially manufactured over heat in a test tube.

This part of the house is very awkward to get to which is why I come here, as I rarely get disturbed. Having made the steep ascent up the spiral staircase, you then have to take your life in your hands and cross a rotten attic floor full of holes, climb backwards out of a window and descend a rickety wooden ladder (which for every rung has two missing) out onto the leads. The dogs are whining at the window because I am out of sight and the ladder is beyond even their capabilities. I love being up among the chimneys, with the house stretching out like a town around me – it gives me a quite inexplicable feeling of superiority. But not today. Today I feel beleaguered. And when I feel beleaguered this is where I come – because it is wonderfully private up here. I am only visible to things that can fly. The leads are deliciously warm; my calves, I notice, are reddening up beautifully. A very interesting variety of insect, of a kind you don't normally see on the ground, has suddenly taken an interest in my legs, so I shall have to hop up onto the wall if I am to get any peace.

I have come up here to write. I find it is easier to look back on life if I am elevated. My feeling of beleaguerment stems from an incident involving a shrew and a bed and breakfast guest. I realise that an extraordinary leap of faith is required to accept that we are now in a position to take in paying guests, given the state of the house. But it is true – although sometimes even I find it difficult to believe, particularly after this morning's embarrassment.

We have managed to make the west wing presentable. It is quite cut off from the semi-dereliction of the rest of the house and has its own staircase; and providing people don't maraud into uncharted territory, it is possible (if you narrow your eyes) to imagine that you're staying in a tolerably well-run establishment. Well, it is now. In the beginning there was no fooling anybody. It transpired that our ideas of comfort were very different from everyone else's.

Hard as it is, with the chirruping of summer things all around and the scent of grass clippings and baked gravel floating upwards on the heat-rippled air, it is necessary to go back into the gloom of winter for a moment to explain how we came to be doing bed and breakfast. It all started when Peter announced that he was tired of putting up an endless stream of our friends' teenage daughters and that it was about time those who hadn't come to help started paying for the privilege of being waited on hand and foot. The Bill Weaver experiment had also fuelled the idea to some degree, and this little acorn shot up into a sapling overnight and the whole focus of the restoration of the west wing changed in favour of how best we could comfortably accommodate two couples, maximum.

The Duke of Beaufort's Chamber and the King's Room, within the west wing, were potential candidates for *chambres d'hôte*. How grand those names sounded! The reality, of course, was quite different – the rooms were all red hat and no drawers, as my mother would say. The Duke of Beaufort's Chamber, or the 'Dook's Room' as many of our American guests now call it, was an open-plan area at the top of the back staircase. It required two walls to close the room in as it was originally, a new ceiling (the current one was held up with steel props in three places) and a fireplace – Arthur Clegg had left us with another special edition dating from the 1950s.

The King's Room had the look of a church hall about it. The arched heads of the mullioned windows had somehow survived the fire of 1922 but all the internal partitions had vanished. It was now one large sweep of room, in which echoes bounced like squash balls off the rubble walls. There was a cherry tree outside the window. On summer evenings, occasionally, a nightingale sang from its pearly branches. In winter the rooks cawed from it and from the window you could see thin shimmers of breath rising from their mouths.

It was November: a cruel month, I always think. The countryside was still – poised – as though everything that moved was trying its best to conserve energy. Work on the west wing was lagging behind. Syd and the Scouse Git had finished the roofing work and the partition walls were up where they needed to be, but otherwise the inside resembled a gutted fish: no plumbing, wiring, or plaster on the walls, just an empty, hollowed-out middle with a few stringy entrails hanging loose. Despite Will having extended his working day to a three-and-a-half-hour shift in the late evening, progress was resolutely slow. Numerous strangers would frequently show up at the door: 'Will about?' they'd ask and that was that, he'd be gone for another week laying a patio or unblocking drains on his brother's campsite. He wouldn't be tethered to any job. He was like one of his stone-willed old sheep that kept breaking out through the iron bedstead in the hedge. You turned your back and the next minute he'd be gone, his little red van disappearing up the back road to Betws with three bales of straw tied to the roof rack.

I had an idea that we'd get this job finished in a finger-click if we had a deadline to work towards. Focuses the mind, I thought. So, I took a bed and breakfast booking for the Christmas holiday just to speed things up a little, just to set the cat among the turtle doves. I telephoned the tourist office in Betws-y-Coed and told them we had a vacancy. The lady who enquired sounded genuinely distressed when I had told her we wouldn't be ready to accept guests before Christmas.

'Oh, but you're just what I'm looking for,' she said, 'somewhere quiet and characterful where I can get away from the whole Christmas thing. You see, I've just split up from my husband, and my son and I are desperate to get right away from it all and go somewhere totally different.'

Different it most certainly was, I assured her.

'Oh, please could we come?' a hint of desperation creeping into her voice. 'We wouldn't be any trouble at all, I promise you that. We'd even help cook the Christmas dinner.'

Christmas dinner? Now, I hadn't got beyond the bed bit yet, not to mention the breakfast, and suddenly there was talk of Christmas dinner. My self-assertion vanished in the face of an authoritative older woman. Say no, I kept telling myself, just say no, and then to my surprise I heard myself saying, 'Well in that case, of course you must come.' There was something about her voice. She sounded so nice, so hurt by life and yet so reasonable.

'See you Christmas Eve, then. We'll look forward to it,' I said.

'Will we?' said Peter when I shared the glad tidings with him. 'Will we look forward to sharing our Christmas dinner with two total strangers? I think not.'

Will took the news calmly when he heard that both rooms needed finishing for Christmas. He removed a cigarette from behind his ear, lit it, narrowed his eyes and said, 'Serious,' pronouncing it 'sirius', like the star. 'Major contract,' he said, shaking his curls. 'I can't promise anything.'

'Oh please promise,' we pleaded.

'It's my ewes, see. They've started lambing early this year.'

Our approach to the restoration of the west wing was different from the rest of the house. The main house, being so much older than the west wing, had to look as Sir John Wynn remembered it, when Good Queen Bess was upon the throne. So if, at a moment's notice, he were to step over the petal-strewn threshold, there would be no jarring anachronisms to raise an eyebrow. But this later wing could afford us some play. Bar windows and walls, the fire of 1922 had largely reduced it to a blank canvas and the look of it was entirely a matter of personal choice.

First, though, we needed plaster on the walls. It was in the King's Room that I first learnt to plaster. If you wanted to achieve that slightly dilapidated, uneven look to your plaster finish, you asked an amateur like me to do it. Peter was ahead of me in the plastering stakes, though his skill lay in the minute repairs of medieval wall paintings, not the great sweep of rubble which stretched like a cathedral interior around us. We used a lime mix, of course, with a dash of cow hair to bind it all together, purloined by Will from don't ask where. You pushed the lovely creamy mix well into the interstices of the wall, smearing upwards always, until the wrists began to ache and the lime stingingly rekindled those old, nearly healed cuts. Day by day, the layers built up until the stones were smoothed out; but not entirely – therein lay the difference between the professional and the amateur plasterer. The professional would attempt to flatten the history right out of those walls whereas we aimed to follow the contours of the wall with the trowel, as they did in the old days, allowing the soft undulations to grin through like tumuli in a snowy landscape. And finally the last layer was applied – the thin layer of almost neat lime which you polished with the trowel until it glistened like a veneered tabletop. This was the hardest application of all because any mistakes, any streaks or marks made by the trowel, would set in the plaster for ever.

Ceilings were another matter altogether. We left the

ceilings to the professional, though 'professional' was not a word that immediately came to mind when I saw Will bouncing about on a bridge of bowing scaffolding planks ten feet up in the air. In fact it was altogether too nerve-wracking to watch. The ceiling in the King's Room was regally tall; Will was Celtically short. He needed to get from one end of the ceiling to the other with a continual swipe of plaster, so the deck was constructed to span the length of the room. He ran along the boards as though along a tightrope, eyes and trowel raised to the ceiling. If he were to miss his footing once . . . But it was the same with the chimneys. I had already seen him climb three rickety ladders tied together with baling twine to reach the very top of a chimney stack, with a roll-up glued to his lower lip and a slate crenellation strapped to his back about the size and weight of a filled lavatory cistern. Believe me, the circus was a dull show in comparison.

All the right permissions, such as Listed Buildings Consent, had been sought before removing Arthur Clegg's fireplaces. Though in fact we didn't remove, we merely built over, in case the 1940s – God spare us – should ever come back into vogue. I make note of it here in case future generations of restorers are tempted to peek – I'd say don't bother – let the dead bury the dead. We chose an elegant bolection-moulded number to take its place, which Peter marbled with a peacock feather. He painted the wood to imitate black marble with green veins running through it. At first it looked like a piece of Stilton, but once the finishing streaks had been applied it was an amusing illusion to have your knuckles knock against wood instead of stone.

Gradually, the room was being transformed. We had dissected the space by a third to create a bathroom on one side and a hallway on the other. The bedroom took up the remaining two-thirds. Our local architectural salvage-monger had yielded an old lavatory with overhead cistern called 'The Adamant'. My mother had a ginormous bathtub knocking about in an outhouse, complete with marble-surround. 'That'll do nicely,' I said.

'A kiss and it's yours,' she said, winking.

What was it about plumbers that made them a race apart? It was the first time we'd used anyone out of the phone book. They came, they conquered, they went. Sizewell B might have afforded them more interest. 'It's just a job, love. Who shall I make the invoice out to?' I supposed there was not much excitement to be had out of a copper pipe. Still, the job was done and when we turned on the tap a second miracle in motion flowed forth. The bath was so big you could float in it. And when we pulled the lavatory chain, a thin drizzle of water issued out of the overhead cistern. 'Leave it,' we told the plumbers. Jerry-plumbing was a must in an old house.

The room had progressed beyond the larva stage; the pupa was almost in sight. It was a room that was beginning to unfurl its wings. The hours were ticking down the days to Christmas Eve, only two weeks to go. While we waited for the plaster to dry, we erected the bed. It was another of our home-made affairs. Four rough-sawn posts from the timber yard were neatly chamfered and covered, fairly convincingly by me, in a rich cream brocade. Who was to say it was not a seventeenth-century bed beneath the fabric? Fabric

disguised a multitude of disparities in this house. This time
we chose crewel work for the hangings. We bought it by the
bale from our local remnant shop and had it made into
hangings by Pat, our local needlewoman, who later said in
her quiet Yorkshire brogue, 'I'll not charge thee for my work.
I love what you're doin' at the castle and I'll not charge thee.
It's the least I can do.'

Bless Pat. Those little monkeys on the crewel work
skipped and danced their way to the King's Room. It was
those touches of kindness that kept us on the right track
always: like the donation of fifty pounds from the
Abersoch Women's Institute because they had enjoyed
their visit to the house so much; and the continual stream
of encouragement that flooded through the visitors' book:
'Keep up the good work, this is the best castle ever'. And
from another entry, 'You've taken our breath away'. So
much goodwill, in fact, it made us blush – for weren't we
lucky enough to be doing what we loved most in all the
world?

It was only the bureaucrats who made our journey
difficult – those spiteful pedants who reign supreme in
darkened offices. 'Your garden wall is a danger to the
highway, please get it repaired immediately', etc, etc, while,
letting their own walls fall down twenty feet away. Still, no
matter, let us build up the walls, we said, if only to keep out
the bureaucrats.

It was impossible to forget that Christmas Eve was but
three days away. The little square in Llanrwst pulsated with
Slade's 'Merry Christmas Everybody' and the girls behind
the counter in the bank wore tinsel in their hair. A tractor

pulled a sleigh round the narrow streets and the passing onlookers shouted 'Hi, Brian' to Father Christmas before crossing the road to avoid the chinking bucket.

Three days away and still the walls in the King's Room were nude, without colour. Three days away and it was neither furnished, polished nor swept; and the rush matting lay in a disconsolate roll by the door. And why? Because the plaster was still too damp to paint. Only one thing for it: we attacked the walls with hairdrier and blowlamp. Small square by small, infinite square, the plaster began to lighten as the moisture (and how much moisture there was!) gradually took its leave of the lime. It was not an ideal system but it worked. Chocolate and bananas washed down by mug after mug of hot, rich tea sustained us through the small hours.

At five o'clock in the morning, we were throwing a tinted limewash at the walls. The surface sucked up the ochre pigment like litmus paper. In the 'old days' they used to apply limewash stripped to the waist. I could see why. It was as thin as single cream and had a will of its own. You tried to guide it vaguely with a brush but then it was off where it liked, running down the back of your hand and into your sleeve, gumming up your watchstrap and the laces of your shoes. We were both caked with crusted paint by the time dawn broke through the cherry tree. When it dried it made your skin feel like sun-bleached newspaper. The dogs looked as though they'd been dipped in batter.

We snatched a quick nap, then rushed the rush matting to the floor, upended the bed – heave, over, under, back down – and fixed the hangings. Red velvet curtains. Four lamps. Two upholstered wing-backed chairs on either side of the fireplace. A tallboy between the windows. Pictures: a print of the *Last Supper* in a burr-walnut frame and some dark atmospheric oil of an unknown gentleman. An indecipherable scene on a tapestry above the fireplace. Towelling bathrobe behind the door, some Floris soap in a china dish. Electric blankets on the beds. Plugged-in heaters turned to overdrive.

It was 4pm on Christmas Eve. Just time enough to wash and shop for breakfast, dinner, tea. But we'd done it. Both rooms were complete and ready to receive guests. Imago had occurred; the rooms were in full flight now. And providing no one leaned against the paintwork, all would be well. No amount of money could have bought this moment of satisfaction.

Downstairs, a fire crackled festively in the grate – we'd even saved some extra-dry logs for the occasion and the halls were decked with berryless boughs of holly. It had been a hard winter and the birds had beaten us to the choicest branches. The day before, Peter went outside with an axe and chopped down a fir sapling that had seeded too close to the house. It was a scrawny thing but it served as a Christmas tree of sorts. I had to wire on extra limbs with coat-hanger wire to make it look less of a mongrel, more of an aristocrat among trees; and now it sat in a lead cistern, in the corner of the Lower Hall, looking rather pleased with itself in its newly tinselled attire.

A thin mist of frankincense lingered in the halls. Peter had changed into a jacket and tie. I'd done what I could with myself, but there was very little to go on. 'Have I got black on my face?' I asked Peter. He spat on a tissue and rubbed at a mark on my forehead. It occurred to me that we were nervous.

Our antediluvian fridge groaned with food: turkey, cranberry sauce, Stilton, and so on. There was even a drinks tray laid out on a coffer. Will was putting the last few scaffolding poles into the back of his van. There was nothing for it but to sit and wait. We slumped by the fire, heads propped on hands, too tired to speak, too tired even to rescue the log that rolled forward in the grate.

Next thing we were jumping awake. It was black outside; the fire had gone out and the candles had all burnt down. Hell, what time was it? It was eight o'clock! No sign of our guests. Strange. They said they'd be here at six. We gave them the benefit of holiday traffic and shrugged. 'Like a sherry?' asked Peter.

'Oh, go on, then.' After the fourth tumblerful we'd perked up a lot – hardly the same people, in fact. We'd relaxed into a soporific fug of rosy cheeks and shared cheer. 'Perhaps you'd better phone to see when they left,' said Peter with a contented sigh. Reluctantly, I heaved myself out of my chair. In order to reach the telephone upstairs, it was necessary to pass through a short, near-subterranean passageway and a hall in which the wind-chill factor was evident by the hoary patterns of frost which glazed the inside of the windows.

I dialled. You can imagine the veil of incomprehension that passed over my face when I heard Mrs Clarke's voice at the other end of the line, saying, 'Oh dear. Silly me, didn't I phone to let you know we weren't coming? How very scatterbrained I am.' 'How very scatterbrained.' I mouthed the words. How very scatterbrained indeed, Mrs

Clarke. I wanted to say: 'Have you any idea what we've been through to get those rooms finished in time for you? Just look at these blisters! Just look at the worn knees of my trousers!' A teary tremolo of exhaustion quivered in my throat. I was speechless, with an emotion that was two stabs away from burning red-hot fury. 'A pox on your house, Mrs Clarke!' I wanted to say, but instead I heard my mouth betraying my heart, as it is apt to do under such circumstances. 'You have a Happy Christmas, too,' it said. And then I was replacing the receiver and flying downstairs to tell Peter the news that Mrs Clarke and her son wouldn't be coming after all.

Well, after that there was nothing for it but to drink the rest of the sherry. That took the edge off our disappointment in a big way. I think we might even have laughed a little towards the end of the bottle. It was getting close to midnight and the bells of St Grwst's church were ringing out across the dark enfolding blackness of the valley, calling the town's faithful to prayer. What else but Midnight Mass on Christmas Eve? It was suddenly imperative that we attend. We stepped out in our winter wrappings into the sobering chill of the night only to be transported into a faery paradise of glistening snow. It had snowed to a depth of about three inches while we had been toasting the night inside. The yew trees were lined like a parade of ghosts against the sky and the branches of the cedars bore the whiteness stoically. It was a night that called for a sleigh pulled by black ponies, a rug to wrap over our knees, and Turkish delight to eat. But instead we made do with our own two feet. And it was very lovely indeed to walk arm in arm down the Gwydir avenue with the snow catching on our eyelashes.

As we were taking Communion in church, I couldn't help noticing that we smelt exactly like the old hassocks we were kneeling upon: that clouding smell, damp, with perhaps a bit of civet thrown in for good measure; basically, how you'd smell if you'd been locked in a crypt for twelve years. It was as though we'd been left to soak in an oak-aged vat of Gwydir's perfume.

That Christmas turned out all for the good in the end. Everyone thought we were tending to Mrs Clarke's needs and we were left quite alone in the house. We listened to music, read our Christmas books by the fire and carved small notches of meat out of the overcooked turkey whenever we felt hungry. At night we'd climb into the new bed in the King's Room and fall asleep with the electric blanket on, which made me dream I was crisping up nicely in one of those fiery hell scenes by Hieronymus Bosch.

The snowfall gave us a lovely, legitimate reason to shun society for a while. Sven had gone home to his aged mother for Christmas. A partial collapse in the roof of the coach house had sent the Busbys back to the comforts of Blaenau Ffestiniog. And there was no talk of them coming back either. Gravity had enacted its own eviction of sorts. And we were grateful for it. In recent weeks, the coach house had begun to resemble an overcrowded doll's house. You opened the door and oversized people – previously unknown to us – came tumbling out. It was a relief, at last, to have Gwydir completely to ourselves. We saw no one in fact until New Year's Eve.

I couldn't remember the last time we'd been out together to a party. We'd been invited to a neighbour's house for dinner and it gave me the oddest sensation to be out of wellingtons. It was as though my feet suddenly wanted to float off on their own; it was like walking on clouds. Peter had to exhume his dinner jacket from a tea chest in the attic. It still had a rose in its lapel from the last time he'd worn it to a friend's wedding in London. Another world, another lifetime away. It was a white rose, faded with age to sepia at its heart. A moth had been at the crotch of his trousers but it was too late to do anything about it, so I promised I'd give him a signal whenever the hole became visible. It was the first time we'd left the house alone and it was only when we came to lock up that we realised we didn't have a key. We had locking bars and huge bolts – but no key. Peter rushed off into the night to fetch a ladder. The snow was falling heavier than ever, casting that blue light which made the shadows deeper and the walls of the castle taller. I froze in my thin party clothes. Whoever designs clothes these days ought to spend a few nights in a Tudor castle before making any rash decisions about design over function. Peter had to run round bolting all the doors from the inside and then climb out of an upstairs window in his dinner jacket and dress shoes, looking every bit like Raffles on a job. His silk scarf kept getting tangled in the rungs of the ladder and it was all I could do to stand on the bottom rung and try to prevent the ladder from slipping. It did once, but mercifully an ancient rose hook in the wall prevented a catastrophe. And then Peter had to repeat the whole performance again to get back in – only the dogs made it ten times more difficult the second time, as they would keep showering him with kisses as he tried to climb in through the window.

I can't now remember our first paying guest. Must have come and gone in an interval of held breath. I've got plenty of freeze-framed episodes to call upon, though. I've only to plunge my hand into the tombola of random selection and out come the images by the mindful.

It was easy to forget what an impression the house could make on people. Our guests would often arrive at night. There were no outside lights, just the blackout cloth of the ineffable dark and the squeal of the gate's hinges. The temptation always was to ham it up and say, 'You rang?' But the look on those startled faces was generally enough to temper the theatricals. They were spooked even before they'd entered the courtyard.

The authorities, in their wisdom, have taken away the experience of the night from most people, with their insistence on putting street lights everywhere, and you could see it came as a shock to most to discover the meaning of true darkness. A thin, weary torch beam led them to the door of the Lower Hall. The door, reluctantly, allowed entry with a heavy groan and into the gloom we would plunge. Though secular, it is a strangely hallowed space; spooky, yes – the candles burning, the fire aglow, the monkish music, the dramatic drop in temperature. The stunned silence, always.

And then there's the spiral staircase to negotiate by candlelight. Imagine the wife who totters in on high-heeled shoes, the sort of woman who's gone blonde with age and with a tan that makes you think the rotisserie got jammed. Husband puts his shoulder to it while I pull her up by the hand. After a momentary logjam about halfway up, involving her behind and a leopard-print suitcase, she explodes into the Hall of Meredith with the force of a champagne cork. She has cobwebs in her hair and I can't help noticing a smudge of soot down the back of her white trousers. The stately gloom is almost palpable. The candles dance in the draught and the shadows beat time against the walls.

'I hope to God there's a bar 'ere,' she says in a loud aside. We click-clack across the boards until one heel gets stuck. That's it as far as she's concerned. She's hopping around the Hall of Meredith on one foot, shouting, 'Where the bloody hell have you brought me to this time, Neil?' Peter emerges out of a side door and I swear her feet do actually leave the boards. Madoc meanwhile (who never misses such an opportunity) thrusts his nose into the nether regions of her skin-tight trousers, making her gyrate across the hall as if she's having an attack of St Vitus' Dance. And then, as if to put the final dab of sealing wax on the deed of total sabotage, the bats decide to enter stage left. Oh yes, in they come like little Spitfires, never ones to be left out of an occasion.

'What the . . . ?' her voice trails like a damp firework as she glances up at the roof.

'Birds,' says Peter quick as a flash, 'how on earth did they get in?' I shrug.

'Can't think. I must have left the door open.' An Oscar-winning performance, if I say so myself.

'Bloody funny, birds at this time of night,' says the husband, bringing up the rear. But his wife has bolted for the door and all that remains of her is a white, high-heeled shoe lodged between the floorboards.

Peter and I exchange anxious glances and, sensing trouble ahead, make an executive, telepathic decision to upgrade them to the King's Room. The high ceiling, the huge four-poster bed, the tapestries – all make for a greater impact on entry. We needn't have bothered. There's only one thing on her mind and that's finding out where the minibar lives. A thorough and ultimately fruitless search of the room begins.

'Now,' says husband, struggling in with her remaining wardrobe. 'Where's the television lounge?'

'Television lounge?'

'You've got tellies, I take it?'

'No, we haven't got tellies,' I say, not meaning to sound apologetic.

'You mean I can't watch the World Cup tonight?'

'Looks that way,' says Peter.

'Right, well that's that then. Rita, come on, we're going.'

And that *was* that. We performed the whole pantomime in reverse, dislodging the shoe as we went, accompanied by a litany of disgruntled mutterings from Mr Disgusted, while his wife swung her handbag over her head to keep the bats at bay.

Granted, that one was a particularly bad experience for us – and them. On the whole, however, most of our guests get the point completely. Where else, for example, can people breakfast by a roaring fire in one of the finest great halls in Wales? Where else can they experience that truly authentic feeling of never having enough hot water to bathe in? Where else can they watch bats perform from the comfort of their own fireside chairs? And only this morning, a small American child found a shrew at the bottom of her bath and we were able to rehouse it in the garden in double-quick time before her mother saw it. I bribed the child with a peacock feather to keep her quiet and all was well until the shrew bit her finger on departing for the undergrowth.

14
A Woman's Work

I wonder who actually said a woman's work is never done? It must have been a woman; and she was right, of course. Apart from my bookbinding, this house demands that I am all things to all people: cook, secretary, gardener, nurse; and, out of hours, if one consults the annals of housewifery, my duties as a hostess are not to be neglected either.

In the old days (and by old days I mean all periods before the eighteenth century, when people still believed in magic) the mistress of the house had an essential role to play. You get the feeling Gwydir might have collapsed like a house of cards had it not been for its mistress's guiding hand. Throughout the ages, not only did she see to the running of the house but her husband often deferred to her reasoned judgement in estate matters. And yet as confidante, pharmicist, ambassador, perfumer and mother to all, her story is frequently lost in the patriarchal shadow of his-story.

My Elizabethan counterpart goes quietly about her duties. Let us first accompany her to the still room. This room is solely her domain. She keeps the key on a long chain that falls from her waist and no one is allowed to enter without her prior knowledge. Herbs hang in bunches from iron hooks in the ceiling and the walls are lined with shelves that hold tall, narrow-necked phials and alembics filled with scented elixirs and vermilion-coloured liquids. The room is kept warm so that the herbs will release their healing bounty more readily. Where the sun falls across the floorboards, large earthenware crocks contain a concoction of root of angelica and white wine vinegar, which she will use to purify the air of her chamber. Nearby, another deep basin contains a steeping mixture of rhubarb and white wine, which she will later use to colour her hair. It is a paradise for the senses, with that dark edge of mystery that you often find in a room exclusively used by a woman. The scent of orris root and myrrh linger in the folds of her skirts and to find oneself caught in her slipstream as she crosses the house is to imagine oneself cast on a journey to the Orient.

There is a small copper still, in the corner of the room, from which essences are extracted drop by precious drop. After years of use, the worktable is as blond as our mistress's hair and upon it are ranged mortars and pestles of varying sizes where she grinds up the herbs to make her potions and unguents that will safeguard the health of her household – siblings and servants alike.

In the still room she will also concoct the perfumes that will 'make faire' all the rooms in the house. She will make washballs and candles, sweet-smelling vinegars and seasonings for cooking. And she will make the tussie-mussies her sons will clutch to their noses in London's stinking, plague-ridden streets. These delicately perfumed nosegays hold a special place in her affections, for didn't she hook her husband with a tussie-mussie? The secret language of flowers speaks volumes when exchanged with another: fennel for flattery; pansies for courtship; daisies for wantonness; basil for love.

All these recipes she records in a leather-bound book in her careful, slanting hand. She writes: 'take the flowres of rosemary or lavender and put them in a chest amonge your clothes or amonge bokes and moths shall not hurte them'. There is a recipe for white plum cake and 'calfes head pye', and hidden carefully in the back of the book beneath a leather flap is a recipe to 'enable ye to see fairies'.

Some of these recipes have been passed down from the ancients who knew that strong, clean scents kept illness and insects away. The word 'perfume' comes from the Latin, 'through smoke', and frequently she will fumigate her clothes with scented resins to keep out the lice.

At the end of the day, she gets up from her work and goes to the casement which overlooks the little herb garden – some lumps in the lawn are all that remain of it now. Her simples – or medicinal herbs – are almost ready for picking. She knows the best time to harvest is just after the dew was dried on a warm sunny morning, before the flower heads drop their petals. She knows which leaves will yield the best fragrance by their colour alone because this sort of knowledge is bred in the bone.

I'm certain I have the genetic imprint of the still room upon me. I can't forget what it is to smell herbs infusing on a warm day or that piquant aroma of lemon verbena being ground to a soft pulp between mortar and pestle. One day soon I mean to have my own still room in the house. I've got my eye on a chamber at the top of the Solar Tower; but first it needs reroofing, repointing and reglazing. There's always a myriad different jobs that need doing before the end result can be realised. I have an idea that my still room will evolve into a bit of an alchemist's laboratory where I can spend the next fifty years in quiet pursuit of the philosopher's stone. Gwydir had one once. Sir Owen Wynn, the third baronet, was an alchemist. His collection of alchemic books are listed in an inventory of 1635. It includes such delicious titles as the *Mirrour of Alchymie* and *The Magneticke Cure of Wound*s.

And next door to the still room we intend to have a *Wunderkammer* – a walk-in cabinet of curiosities popular in the seventeenth century – which will almost certainly terrify the young and will no doubt make the old assume we are necromancers. There will be crocodiles hanging from the ceiling and exotic shells and precious stones ranged on shelves against the walls, and lots of two-headed things in jars and all manner of tusks and probosces. Gwydir had all these things once and it seems only right that it should have them again.

In the meantime, while I await the arrival of roof, walls and doors, I am forced to enact my still-room experiments upon the kitchen table. I attempt to make soap. There is an easy way and a difficult way to make soap. Naturally, the difficult way comes first. Ever the purist, I choose to make it as Lady Sydney Wynn might have done in about 1580. I take eight cups of wood ash out of the fire, as the recipe suggests. I put the ash in a large crock, cover it with boiling water and allow it to steep for ten days. Then I separate the water and throw away the wood ash. The watery paste is called lye and the surprising thing is, it feels soapy. Next you melt lamb fat on a low heat and then add about half a cup of lye to the pot. It's about this point that you wish you'd never started the whole procedure. The thought of applying this greasy, gungy, lamb-dinner-scented concoction to the skin, to make it clean, sends contra-positive messages to the brain. Still, having come this far you press on, regardless of the fat that is congealing in white flecks all over the stove. The mixture cools and then you add a perfume of your choice, and this is interesting because as soon as something smells nice, suddenly it's somehow not so repellent – ergo, the evidence of the nose is more compelling than the eye. I choose essence of rose with a dash of patchouli and a frisk of peppermint oil. You then pat it into moulds and let it dry for about a month. The whole operation takes about six weeks in all to complete and you're left with a crusty presentation bar that takes your skin off if you rub too hard.

An easier way is to buy unscented soap flakes, heat them up on the stove, add a handful of oatmeal, a cup of rosewater and a slurp of avocado oil. Allow the ingredients to cool, then mix in a blender and, finally, add five drops of lavender oil. An easier way still is to go to a shop, choose from an array of about fifteen different soaps, pay for it and then come home again. It doesn't give you that same sense of satisfaction, but it's certainly gentler on the purse and the cooking utensils in the long run.

I thought of setting up a castle industry on the back of my success in the soap-making field. But there were 'unknown quantities' at work which I hadn't taken into account, such as what happens if you wrap soap in cellophane when it hasn't dried out properly. Well, I'll tell you what happens: it sweats like a steaming tea bag, which makes the rose petals that have gone into decorating the soap rot down to a mouldy pulp inside the moisture-condensing cellophane. Hardly conducive to the purchasing allure of a luxury product. I'd already sold a few bars by the time this started happening, but by then it was too late for a product recall.

I also tried my hand at making my own scented candles and pot-pourri because the house seemed to rebel, as did Peter, against any smell that came out of an aerosol can. There were pots full of urine-coloured liquid steeping under staircases; there were trays of rose petals desiccating in silica gel on every available window sill. The house lapped up those dusty scents of old summer; and by the time I'd worked through my book of still-room recipes, I had a fair idea how our Elizabethan mistress might have spent her days at Gwydir.

She rises with the sun, pulls open the yellow damask curtains of her bed and is greeted by her maidservant, Mally, who is a girl of gentle birth pleased to serve her. On cold days, the fire in her chamber has already been lit; the room is warm. Still in her shift, she sits for Mally who combs out the tangled, golden tresses of her hair each morning. Hair-fixing takes the longest time of all and it is hard not to become impatient for the pulling to cease and the black cap to be pinned in place upon her head. Next, she blackens her eyebrows with kohl, applies white lead to her face, uses fucus to rouge her cheeks and belladonna to enlarge the size of her eyes. Her chamber is by now already thick with perfume. The clothes she wears about the house are usually simple and black, for most of her adult life has been spent in mourning for the sons she has outlived. She leaves her shift in place, puts on a stomacher, a black velvet bodice and a skirt which falls over a farthingale, allowing her, at last, free use of her hands after centuries of picking up her train to stop it trailing in the dirt on the flagstones. Her cuffs are trimmed with lace and around her neck she wears a large pleated ruff which is fixed with wire at the back. She steps into black silk slippers adorned with little silk rosettes and finally she hangs about her neck a miniature of her dear husband dangling on a long crimson ribbon.

Her days are full. When she is not in her still room, she might work at her books with an assortment of gentle-women who have entered her service to be taught the skills of housewifery: reading, needlework, musical accomplish-ment and dancing, in the hope that better manners will be passed on to them. She teaches them how to stand, when to rise, how deep to make a curtsy, and the correct way of sneezing.

Once a day she will attend prayers given by John Price, the house chaplain, but throughout the day her private devotions will continue and her psalter (for which she has made an embroidered cover) is kept near at hand. Sometimes, on fine days, she will accompany her husband out hunting in the forests or she will watch him partake of a game of bowls on the green, which still survives, though much overgrown now, in the woods above Gwydir. Sweetmeats will be served, as well as pickled walnuts and oysters, and tall fluted glasses filled with sweet sack.

In the afternoons, when she is not bestowing charity upon the poor at the almshouses her husband has built, she plays the virginals. She can sing tolerably well too; but her favourite pastime is reading. She spends hours with her books, reading French romances and Ovid, Cicero and Plutarch. And she is more comfortable now that she no longer has to sit of an evening in the draughts of the Great Hall, for times are changing and smaller upper chambers are more congenial with their wall chimneys and glass windows, instead of the open central hearth of her grandmother's day, which filled the room with smoke.

The kitchen is not a room she ventures into often. While she agrees the menus (always careful to avoid food that might bring on her husband's bilious attacks), other people prepare and chop, and stoke the ovens. But in the still room she will supervise the brewing which produces the ale for dinner and supper. Breakfast is a simple repast; with dinner being the main meal of the day, served around midday. It will often consist of two or three courses, sometimes with twenty small dishes at each course. Supper is a smaller meal and will be served in the late afternoon. Afterwards, her husband will take his tobacco whether 'he needs it or no' and she will take a pinch of powdered ancient mummy in a herbal tisane which the physicians claim will keep her youthful.

In homage to the Elizabethan kitchen we once cooked a peacock – a great delicacy in the sixteenth century. It was a sad affair seeing that noble bird discarded on the side of the road after a hit-and-run incident, limp necked, its white lids closed over its eyes. We plucked it and then wrapped its head and neck in a damp towel to preserve its feathers, as the recipe dictated. It looked like a big goose or a Christmas turkey. But the trouble was we knew it wasn't

– it was dear Cassandra – and when it came down to it, we could no more eat her than we could fly. We gave her a state funeral, giblet gravy and all, in the Commemorative Garden and Peter erected a stone to her memory, lest we forget.

If the testimony of the bards is anything to go by, there were some strong-minded wives here at Gwydir during the Elizabethan period – strong-minded to the point of selflessness, one might say today. We already know about Margaret's inner strengths but take Lady Sydney Wynn, for example, wife of Sir John Wynn and mother of eleven children. She held the old house together (for it was old even in their day) after her dear husband's death in 1627. Though it was in the house-bard's interests to say nice things about his benefactress, Huw Machno did say that Lady Sydney was the 'gwinllan', the 'vineyard' who kept the whole estate nourished with true goodness and moral fortitude.

And there was Grace Williams, niece of Archbishop John Williams and wife of Sir Owen Wynn, who was charged with looking after Gwydir while his brother Sir Richard was away making a name for himself at court. But Owen, who, we are told, 'always wore his beard careless,' was less inclined to run the estate and more inclined to keep his nose tucked up in his alchemical writings, so it fell to able Grace to run the household. She was, by all accounts, the power behind her less assertive husband. It was Grace who had to deal with the nine hundred ravenous Cavaliers who came knocking at the gates, following the Battle of Denbigh Green, on that fateful night of 1 November 1645. It is not recorded, but doubtless she dealt with the 'unrulies' like a true heroine of any Civil War romance you care to read, even if they did, on leaving, sack the place. But at least they didn't run off with a hundred head of cattle, as the Roundheads had done a few months earlier.

And then there's Katheryn of Berain, cousin of Queen Elizabeth I, who was known posthumously as '*Mam Cymru*' (the 'Mother of Wales') because of the many and various genealogies that sprang from her loins on account of her marrying four times. Four times! Her story upstages every one of her husbands for sheer vibrancy, and it's strangely gratifying to hear of a Tudor girl in charge of her own destiny for a change.

The story goes that Maurice Wynn of Gwydir proposed to her as he led her away from the church at the funeral of her first husband, but she had to refuse him as she had already accepted Sir Richard Clough on her way into the church. She promised, however, that if she were to perform the same sad duty for Sir Richard, Maurice might depend on being the third. Five years later, she buried Sir Richard and married Maurice. Ten years later, she buried Maurice and married again. And one can only imagine that a decent settlement was to be had out of every husband and that a widow's dowry was worth marrying for.

The gossipmongers thought her exploits too good an opportunity to miss and rumour went about that whenever she tired of a lover, she poured molten lead in his ears and buried him in the orchard at Berain, the place of her birth. Her biographer informs us that if there is a grain of truth to be had out of the story, it can only refer to the last ten years of her life, during only part of which she lived at Berain. Gwydir was also famous for its orchards in Maurice's day: they were said to be fertile places where vines and apples grew. Perhaps time has confused its orchards. I say no more.

Her slippers and her corset still reside behind glass in a house in North Wales. We once made a pilgrimage to see them. They were given to her by her godmother, Queen Elizabeth I; the slippers so tiny, so faded, so far away from the myth of her, juxtaposed with the image of the corset which almost brought her bouncing back into the room. Each morning on my way down the spiral staircase I stroke the same door that she, too, would have stroked on her way down to the Lower Hall. I know this, for the door predates her occupation of Gwydir by thirty years. I click the same latch and feel the heavy mass of oak drop slightly on the swing of the same strap hinges. To me, the continuity of such things is reassuring. I am reminded that we are the future the past looked forward to and it gives me reason to hope – though hope, as someone once said, is often the last refuge of the disillusioned.

15

Adventures in New York City

$\mathcal{W}$e stepped out of the refrigerated air of the airport terminal into a warm wall of city fumes and attempted to hail a taxi. Our fellow travellers had a knack of flagging down taxis by throwing out their besuited arms in a confident manner. Our tweed-clad arms didn't quite have the same effect and soon we found ourselves alone outside the concourse of New York's John F. Kennedy Airport. It seemed unreal that we were here to see our panelled room, and the journey, in every sense, had not been without its excitements.

We'd heard nothing from Bill after he left Gwydir that morning except for a polite thank-you note saying what an enjoyable evening he'd had. It wasn't until a few months later that we received a formal letter from him, coincidentally on the same day as the swallows arrived back. And I cried, partly because of the letter, but also because of the swallows and the miracle of their safe return. They gathered in their hundreds, perhaps thousands, high up in the sky looking like television fuzz, as I remembered it, and I wondered whether the fly-past was for our benefit or whether the gathering had some symbolic or procreative meaning. On reflection, it seemed the latter was the more likely.

The letter was as much of a surprise as if the swallows themselves had let it down from the heavens on silk ribbon. It said: 'I am writing to offer you the room from Gwydir Castle'. No smoothing down of the bed sheets there, just straight to the point. I liked Bill for that. He cast this happy grenade into our midst and the explosion was all confetti and church bells. We could hardly believe what we were reading. It continued: 'The Acquisitions Committee of the Board of Trustees have voted to de-accession the room and have provided required notice to the Attorney-General of the State of New York'. The Attorney-General of the State of New York, no less! What had Bill said to sway the trustees in our favour?

But what was this? The room was being offered for *sale*. The rest was an unfocused blur – of terms and conditions of sale and possible shipment dates if the offer proved acceptable to us.

How simple-minded of us not to have imagined that the museum would want some kind of remuneration. Naive in the extreme to imagine that one good cause might just do another a good turn. 'You get nothing for nothing in this life,' said my mother when she heard.

We wrote straight back and said thank you very much, what an extraordinary thing this would be for Gwydir, but we were in no position to pull a gold ingot out of the hat this week, and how about giving it to us on permanent loan instead? The response was polite but firm. Bill packaged up the word 'no' and sent it to us in cotton wool. But it was still *no* when we lifted it out of the box. The trustees had the welfare of the museum to consider, he said, and they had voted for an outright sale.

Now, we were momentarily flummoxed by this. Our finances were not as precarious as they had been, say, a year ago, given that we now had bed and breakfast and public opening to fall back on, but every penny we could make was buying lead and lime and expertise. There was certainly no money to spare for the purchase of a baroque Dining Room, however much we yearned to have it back.

Every evening we would sit in the garden watching the swallows skimming insects off the lawn, like froth off a casserole. The midges began to bite after six o'clock. Someone had told us that elder leaves kept the midges away so we would sit with leafy helmets on our heads, looking like oversized elves in an Arthur Rackham drawing, dreaming up fund-raising ideas to buy our Dining Room back. There was talk of a strawberry tea and Sven thought of a sponsored wheelbarrow push from Land's End to John o'Groats. But really, deep down, we knew we were using a worm to catch a whale. We needed a trawler with an industrial-sized hook to catch a whale of these proportions.

And yet here we were, six months later, on our way to visit the Metropolitan Museum in New York to see the room we were just about to buy. Who would have believed it? Luckily for us, the Welsh Office were feeling flush at the time of our request – different story altogether, now. These days the show is run by accountants and solicitors who are more inclined to tell you that you get nothing for nothing in this world, as my mother had done and an historic house must make its own way in the world. Anyway, we made an impassioned plea to Cadw, the heritage body of the Welsh Office urging them to help us to save this seminally important piece of welsh heritage before the Metropolitan Museum withdrew its offer and it was lost to the nation. It wasn't long before the press sniffed out the story and suddenly one morning we found ourselves in the news: 'Castle Treasure Seekers' ran one headline, 'The Room that Came Out of a Box' ran another, and Cadw, found themselves embraced by the story and with grace agreed to stump up some money in the form of a generous Historic Building Grant.

So here we were at JFK, having stood on the concourse of the airport for a good twenty minutes, until eventually a rusting Cadillac drove by. I waved my old school scarf at the driver but he passed on, and then suddenly had a change of heart, stopped and reversed. Sparks flew off the exhaust pipe as it scraped on the tarmac.

Peter cleared his throat and said: 'Good morning, could you take us to the Pierpont Morgan Library, please?' The driver (of Hispanic descent, I think) stared blankly at us. Peter pulled out a crumpled bit of paper from his inside jacket pocket and showed him the address.

'Ah, *si*,' he said. The back door of the car was jammed, so the driver got out and kicked it and it opened petulantly with a whine. We sped off at Mach 4 speed, weaving in and out of lanes, with car horns hooting behind us and the radio booming out. It was a harrowing journey. I looked around the car for signs of a taxi licence but there was nothing to suggest our driver was in any way a law-abiding citizen. Finally, we pulled up in some backstreet outside a shop called Morgan's, which sold televisions. Nothing would have made me get back into the cab, so we paid him the equivalent of a week's housekeeping and he sped off yelling (none too politely, I might add) that his tip was an insult and didn't we know he had a family to feed.

We looked around us. Peter couldn't get over the metal

kerbs edging the pavements. Everything felt so early twentieth century somehow. Even the school buses looked like products of the 1930s. There was a man, reading a paper, having his shoes shined on the street corner. The soft, spongy smell of hot dogs carried down the street.

It occurred to us that we hadn't caught sight of a television in over two years. We stood on the sidewalk, hypnotised by the moving pictures in Morgan's shop window. We must have stood there for ten minutes or so, watching *Oprah* and re-runs of *The Waltons*, until we realised we were half an hour late for our meeting with my friend Lilla, who had agreed to put us up during our stay in New York. We dashed off, making the wheels of our suitcase spin over the cracks in the pavement; but we needn't have rushed because, as I had predicted, Lilla was a good hour late herself.

That night, ensconced in her warm, dry, batless house, I stood under the pressure-hose strength of the shower and pondered how much our lives had changed since Gwydir. No one could have predicted how different things would be, but on the face of it there was nothing of the modern world I missed or regretted having lost. I thought of the first generation of Wynns who had crossed the Atlantic and settled in Virginia in the seventeenth century, and wondered what they had made of this land of plenty after the lean pickings of North Wales. Later on in bed I tried to sleep, but this was the first night we had spent away from the castle in over two years and the city was bright in my mind, as though the flashing neon signs of Times Square had got behind my eyeballs and were determined to convert me to the merits of Coca-Cola.

The following day Lilla dropped us off at 1000 Fifth Avenue, outside the Metropolitan Museum. The day, as they say, had finally come. It was just after ten o'clock in the morning and I could already feel the heat from the sidewalk rising up through my shoes. The great classical façade of the museum loomed up in front of us. Standing at the bottom of a sweeping flight of steps, we held hands like two children trembling before the gates of some sultan's palace. It was time to go in. We gave our names at the desk and were given little Ms to pin onto our coats, which made us feel even more like lost property. Then suddenly Bill was beside us, immaculate in his grey suit, welcoming us and asking polite questions about our health and the weather. Once we'd established that we were tolerably well (bar the chilblains) and that the weather was predictably awful back home for the time of year, Bill led us through some double doors behind a scagliola column. I asked him jovially if it would be all right for Lilla to join us at the warehouse later.

He stopped and said in his cool, vowel-elongating drawl, 'My Gaad, I don't think you realise where we're going.' He was right, I didn't have the faintest clue.

'It is no place for a tea party. Ladies do not drive alone through that neighbourhood, let alone stand around on street corners.' Chastened, I fell silent as an image of a Wild West shoot-out played through my mind.

We seemed to walk for miles down white hospital-like corridors, into lifts and out of lifts, through open-plan offices where people charged about with fax messages trailing behind them. On we went, down into the bowels of the building where the mops and the vacuums lived, until at last we arrived in an underground car park. A row of shining vehicles lined the far wall, so shiny in fact that I thought they warranted flags on their bonnets. A group of people with clipboards and walkie-talkies turned to greet us. It was a VIP moment I thought, almost a 'Good morning, Mr President,' moment; but instead they merely asked us whether we wanted coffee from the dispenser. We were introduced to Eric who was built like a centre half, with a Colgate smile that made me reach for my sunglasses. He pinched the rim of his baseball cap and said: 'How you doin'?' and his leather jacket creaked like a rancher's saddle. A huddle of security men loitered nearby and on the fringe of the group two elegantly turned-out women, wearing dark city suits, were engrossed in whispered conversation.

Eric turned to Bill and said, 'What are we taking, chief, the taxi or the ambulance?' Bill told us, for reasons of security, we would be travelling incognito in the ambulance. A silent driver led the way, but Eric hung back mouthing something intently into his walkie-talkie.

'Whoa, hold on, chief, change of plan. Security say we should take the van.' He pointed to a conspicuously new white Ford with black tinted windows.

'Well then, let's go,' said Bill, and suddenly everything began to speed up. We were bustled into the van's carpeted interior. The driver, Eric and Bill piled in after us and the electric doors to the basement were raised. We sped up the ramp and out onto Fifth Avenue. Horns sounded. The great art deco façades flashed by. Traffic signs blinked:

WALK – DON'T WALK. Everyone was curiously silent on the journey, as though wary of eliciting any searching questions from us like: 'Where exactly are you taking us?'

Gradually, the opulent streets became less opulent, more downtown; then gradually less downtown, more down and out. Coils of barbed wire fringed the tops of buildings. Predatory youths on bikes patrolled the streets and steam rose from the drain covers, like a depiction of hell in a medieval painting. We found ourselves in the land of the burnt-out, red-brick tenement. A young black child played with a toy Kalashnikov on the bonnet of a smashed-up Mercedes.

I was finding it increasingly difficult to imagine our room in this loud, sticky city and yet here it had lain for all those years, sealed in its crates, biding its time, awaiting its fate. Bill told us that the Metropolitan kept a number of anonymous warehouses across the city where they stored the objects not chosen for display in the museum – poor objects, I thought, never to feel the warm sun of admiration upon their dusty surfaces, but left to languish for ever in the chill wind of rejection. How happy our room would be, I thought, when it found out it was coming home at last after its seventy-five-year exile.

We pulled up outside a big, ugly warehouse in a sidestreet full of similar blocks. Most of the buildings were derelict, but the odd floor showed valiant signs of occupation: a huge cardboard sunflower face stuck to a window and a line of washing strung between two balconies.

The door of the van slid open. Other than some faded black letters on the side of the building, there were no distinguishing features. The windows on the first floor were blanked out with brown paper.

'Quick, in through the door,' said Eric, and the van sped off. 'You don't want to hang around in this neighbour-hood.'

We were ushered into an old elevator which wheezed its way up several floors. When we reached the tenth floor, the latticed metal door was pulled aside and we emerged into a dingy space that smelt most unappealingly of stale urine and engine oil. The repetitive beat of mechanical noise thundered out below us, as though giant pistons were punching out car parts. Sidestepping a dead pigeon on the stairs, we arrived at a large steel door. Eric produced a loop of keys from his pocket and turned three, well-oiled locks. The door opened heavily, like that to a safe, and an angry alarm whined inside. I moved forward.

'Stay there, please, ma'am,' said Eric. Bill touched my arm lightly. We waited outside while the alarm was demobilised. I suddenly felt nervous, as though I was about to meet some grand old aunt whom I had never met before but had heard so much about. There was also the niggling fear that the room we had travelled three thousand miles to see, would not – for some unexplained reason – be here. When the door opened, the strip lights blinded us momentarily. We stood on the threshold and blinked. Gradually, my eyes adjusted to a strangely familiar scene: a vast warehouse full of thousands of packaged objects. Why was this so familiar? It took me a moment to realise the connection. Of course – we had stumbled into the final scene of *Citizen Kane*, the one where the journalists are searching a crammed warehouse for the secret of 'Rosebud'.

Silhouetted against the far windows was a city-scape of crates, like the Manhattan skyline itself. Life-sized casts of the four horses of San Marco reared up out of a sea of bubble wrap. Giant terracotta urns flanked the entrance to a maze of storage racks; a line of Corinthian columns were laid out on the floor, hidden by dust sheets like a row of dead soldiers beneath palls. Only the objects too big to be wrapped were fully visible. Occasionally, the outer wrapping of some smaller package had been torn to reveal a jewelled casket or a delicate piece of porcelain. Bill led the way down a dusty corridor of packing crates. Labels flapped out towards us. I caught glimpses of accession numbers and the odd tantalising description. A life-sized statue of Poseidon, his trident menacingly poised, loomed down upon us.

Suddenly, Bill stepped to one side. 'After you,' he said, and Peter and I squeezed passed him into a clearing edged by more boxes. The strip light blinked above us.

On the aeroplane coming over, I had read an account of Howard Carter and Lord Carnarvon's discovery of the tomb of Tutankhamun. I recalled the moment when Carter thrust a candle through a hole in the door of the tomb and peered inside. Their words came back to me now as my eyes adjusted to the dingy light of this far corner of the warehouse. When Carnarvon asked Carter what he could see in the tomb, Carter replied: 'I can see wonderful things.' I knew that feeling; I, too, could see wonderful things. There ahead of us were the fourteen crates of Lot

88 – Gwydir's lost treasure. Carter had said that everywhere in the tomb he could see the glint of gold; and so it was for us. Sections of leather frieze stood propped up against the crates and, though dulled by decades of grime, the gold leaf was doing its best to burst through the dirt. A glint of polished wood flashed out of the gloom; the face of a lion stared up at us from a nest of wood straw, and the numerous carved panels – which we had come to know so well from the catalogue photographs – lay half hidden, half submerged, like old wrecks at the bottom of the ocean.

Three crates had been opened in anticipation of our visit, the remaining eleven were intact, still sealed in their original cases from 1921. Eric and Peter carefully set to work with hammer and chisel; and as the nicotine-coloured lid of the first box splintered open, a mushroom cloud of dust rose up. Bill pulled an immaculate silk handkerchief from his top pocket and held it to his nose.

'My God, it even smells of Gwydir!' said Peter, with a look of delighted wonderment on his face. And so it did. Preserved in their crates, the panels still smelt of wood smoke and damp limestone and the ferns which flourished in our cool, green valley, three thousand miles away. We delved into the wood straw as though into a tombola and together pulled out an eight-foot parcel wrapped in yellowed string and brown paper. We tore open the packaging and found a twisted wooden column intricately carved with vine leaves and exotic birds clinging to bunches of grapes. We recognised it immediately to be one of the columns which held up the overmantel of the fireplace. The quality of the craftsmanship was astonishing, far better than we could ever have imagined. Within each crate there was some new and exciting discovery. The sepia photographs had hidden a wealth of detail. The six window shutters were carved with little cherubs cavorting upon the backs of dolphins and diminutive huntsmen chasing giant deer. The door itself (which Eric said would take four men to lift) had a griffin the size of a small dog carved upon it in high relief.

At some later date, perhaps in the nineteenth century, the leather frieze had been stretched out onto flat battens, each sheet measuring approximately six by four feet. With my handkerchief, I carefully rubbed a circle in the dirt and the gold leaf which covered the embossed leather shone through. Its surface was covered with a complex geometric pattern on a gold and silver background.

We had come armed with tape measures and notebooks hoping to measure each piece as it came out of the crates, in order to make a scaled drawing of the room. This would then serve as our blueprint and would allow us to begin work as soon as we returned home. Once every crate had been opened and the wood straw and brown paper had been removed, we calculated that if you counted all the loose pieces of moulding which were sliding about at the bottom of the crates, there were over two thousand pieces of wood which belonged somewhere. In all, there were over six tons of material. The plan to measure and record every piece was soon abandoned in favour of a more general approach to measure just the big bits. We began with the huge ten by eight feet sheets of small-field oak panelling which would eventually sit against the walls of the room.

Eric turned his baseball cap around in anticipation of the effort it would need to raise the first piece from the crate. Bill stepped back. The fabulous weight of the things made them bow in the middle. I crawled underneath and acted as support, while Peter measured and Eric sweated. Over the decades, the summers had softened the varnish and the winters had hardened it. Consequently, a collage of wood straw had adhered itself to the treacled surface. I noticed a few smashed windows at the back of the warehouse and it was also apparent that there was no humidity-control on site. I envisaged it would take several weeks to clean up the panelling before we could even begin to reinstate it. The panels themselves were made from quarter-cut oak and were the colour of plain chocolate. The baroque door-surround alone took up three of the fourteen crates and had been disassembled into over fifty pieces.

We clung to the dim hope of finding some kind of plan or assembly instructions scribbled down on the back of an old Woodbine packet at the bottom of one of the crates. But there was nothing. It was naive of us to have imagined that the whole room would reassemble with the ease of an Ikea flatpack. Our only clues were to be found on the back of each of the larger pieces of panelling. Daubed in white paint were confused references to the position of each piece within the room, such as 'OPP WINDOW SECTION LEFT FLANK MIDDLE' or 'LEFT WINDOW NORTH WALL RIGHT SOFFIT, RIGHT FLANK'. Still, they were clues to be thankful for.

Five hours had passed. My throat was raw with dust, Peter had developed a moustache of dirt, and Bill, by comparison, appeared to have become cleaner.

That evening Bill took us out for an elegant dinner and there was a lovely waiter with a ponytail who kept filling up my glass. Gwydir seemed a lifetime away. I sneaked a look at my watch under the table and counted five hours forward. It would be quite dark at home. In my mind, I saw the moon-washed garden and the slightly chill summer night brightening the stars; the fountain throwing its diamond droplets into the air; and across the blue lawn the shadows of the yew trees strangely elongated, like the kind of hats Cavaliers wore in the seventeenth century. There might even have been a vixen sniffing around the base of the cedar where the peacocks lived, seeing what she might pick up for her children's supper, and perhaps the hedgehogs were already out snuffling for grubs beneath the laurel hedge. Voluptuous tendrils of wisteria would be curling around the window bars, too, carrying into the house a scent as rich as double cream.

My mind sped on through a slide show of images more real to me than the restaurant I was sitting in. It was as though I'd left my heart hanging in a velvet bag from a branch of the Lovers' Tree and every so often I felt it stirring, softly, as though rocked by the wind all those miles away.

16

Standing On Ceremony

I am still up here on the roof and have a perfect view down into the courtyard, while being completely hidden behind the parapet wall. At least I am now in the shade. I have an Elizabethan attitude to the sun: complexions are best kept pale, which is a lucky preference given that the sun is a rare visitor to these parts. Sitting writing up here has made me forget all the things I must accomplish this afternoon.

Peter has just answered the bell and an elderly lady has come in, moving him deftly to one side with her walking stick as though he were a plastic bag stuck on a bramble. She says: 'Young man, do you know who I am?' in an imperious tone one would usually reserve for a wayward spaniel. Incivility, even from the elderly, just doesn't do with Peter. I flinch in anticipation of the acid retort I know must follow.

He says: ''Fraid I haven't a clue. Should I know who you are?'

'Yes, indeed you should. I knew the original owners.'

'Really, you knew Meredith ap Ieuan ap Robert and the fair Alice? That's incredible. You must be at least five hundred years old, in that case.'

I can see them both shooting puzzled glances up towards the roofline at the sound of my giggling, but they don't spot me, which is gratifying, though Peter will have his suspicions as to my whereabouts.

Nowhere in the world could be lovelier than here at this moment. The copper beech is rustling like a crinoline. I can hear the thwack of a cricket ball and the gentle pit-pat of people clapping in the distance. The cricket pitch is just on the edge of the town and the noise carries when the air is as still as it is now. It's lovely when the soccer season finishes and the cricket begins – cricket is more dignified, less tribal somehow. Two turtle doves are pecking away at the peacocks' leftovers in the courtyard. After all the repointing work, the walls of the house are finally beginning to dry out, like sand when the tide recedes. For example, the moss which grows on the inside walls of the Solar Tower has dried out and become furry like 1970s wallpaper and you can now pick it off in gratifying little chunks, which is a good sign. It's wonderful to think of the house being healed by the sunshine.

A Grappolino twin has joined me on the roof. It occurs to me that no one knows this castle better than these cats. Sometimes I wish I could see it through their eyes. Whatever a cranny is, I'm certain we've got plenty for the cats to explore. They must know every inch of the cellars and garderobe shoots, and if Gwydir has a secret room (and Peter is certain it does) they must surely know its whereabouts.

From up here I can see Hazel beavering away in the knot garden. I should be down there with her, but just occasionally it's very restful to knowingly shirk one's duties. Hazel helps us in the garden. She comes all the way from Manchester in her camper van, and in the early days, when funds were at their lowest, she came on a near-voluntary basis just for the sheer love of it. She is about fifty, looks thirty, is quite willowy and walks with the almost imperceptible stoop synonymous with the lady gardener.

Every day we learn something new about the garden.

This week, for example, having filled up the knot garden with a bounteous plenty of herbs (Peter's formality having been relegated to the west side of the house), we discovered – too late – that the peacocks have a particular fondness for fennel, chives, convolvulus and dill. Also, nothing dwarf does well in this garden, as it is just the right size for a peacock to sit on. Things that peacocks don't like are delphinium, lady's mantle, rosemary and periwinkle. I'm sure there must be others, but we haven't found them yet.

I've actually come to rather enjoy gardening in my own way, but I'm not the patient kind of gardener; I like instant rewards. I hate weeding but I love the fast-fix nature of topiary. When I get the clippers out I can't help thinking of Michelangelo 'finding' his David in the block of marble, but unlike him I never know what might come out of the bush to meet me. Yesterday, when I started clipping, I found an enormous rabbit in a ball of box beneath one of the cedar trees. I'm quite pleased with it, though the shape of the ears gave me trouble at the time.

We have also acquired a second-hand sit-on mower to cut the grass, which is proving to be a boon – I do my best thinking while sitting on the mower. Now, what with the new gravel, clipped hedges and cut grass, the gardens are looking quite presentable; though the areas of wilderness are still closest to my heart.

All this activity on the gardening front is in preparation for a wedding. Weddings, like bed and breakfast, were another of those ventures that we rather floundered into, on account of needing to find a way to make more money to finish the gatehouse. This we have now done, but we find we now need money to have the stone mullion window-surrounds cut, which will eventually replace Arthur Clegg's soft-wood frames on the north-facing side of the house. I fear there will never be a time in our lives when we don't need money for some project or other.

We've had a number of weddings already so we know what to expect – only knowing what to expect isn't always a comfort. We now have a licence to conduct civil ceremonies in the Solar Tower. Afterwards, the reception takes place in the Lower Hall.

These days we try our best to discourage people from getting married here, as large parties are apt to become mischievous when under the influence of champagne and sunshine, but a less than positive attitude seems to make people all the more persistent. It's the perfect house for a wedding, after all.

We restrict the festivities to just two rooms in the castle, which is fine providing it doesn't rain. If it rains, we have to creep about on the first floor placing newspapers under the drips – pots and pans are too symphonic and are inclined to drown out the 'I dos'.

A typical wedding ceremony will invariably encompass one or all of the following: Mrs Evans, the local registrar, in her big owl-like glasses, will manage to mispronounce the bride and groom's names; candle wax from the chandeliers will drip onto the best man's tails; one or other of the Grappolini twins will bring a mouse into the hall while the ceremony is taking place and then release it under the bride's mother's folding chair; bride's mother's chair will invariably collapse under the strain of the consequent, vigorous wriggling; a spark from the fire will hop through the fireguard and singe the train of the bride's dress. There is a depressing regularity to two or more of these incidents occurring, no matter what preventative measures we take. As a result, we sit upstairs in a state of high anxiety, waiting for our cue from the caterers (a nice firm from Llanrwst) to come down and stroke the bride's mother back into good humour.

People in a high state of emotion can be very testing at times. Take, for example, the bride's mother who arrived three days early to do the wedding flowers and was still doing them at ten o'clock in the evening when we desperately wanted to go to bed. Like a funeral parlour, the clouding scent of cultivated flowers condensed in the damp, warm air. Unthinkingly (her needs were paramount), she'd plonked several buckets of wet flowers on a 1640s coffer and they'd left dark rings on the lid. Peter was furious, more furious than I ever remembered seeing him, and when he pointed speechlessly to the rings she burst into floods of tears and literally howled, at the top of her voice. The more he tried to get her to stop, the more she howled and then her three friends piled in like Macbeth's witches and began to heckle him for upsetting her.

Then something astonishing happened. Just at the height of the furore, just when the howling was about reaching its crescendo, the lights around the house went out, every one of them – pop, pop, pop. And the room was suddenly plunged into darkness which brought everyone screeching to an abrupt silence. It must have been eerie for those who weren't *au fait* with dark, old, faery castles. A sort of curdled whimper escaped from one of the women. You could have cut their fear with a knife. 'C'mon Sue, we're out of here,' said one of them. Secateurs were dropped, freesias forgotten, and in the beam of a pencil torch they stampeded for the door.

Impossible to say what had happened. It was as though the static charge from the women had backfired and blown the fuse box. Maybe it was just an opportune power cut. Having reset the fuses, the lights flickered on again, but strangest of all, every single clock in the house, wrist-watches and bedside clocks alike, had stopped at ten to ten – just when the lights had blown.

We could have done with a helping hand from the house on the night of the impromptu firework display. Actually, there was nothing *impromptu* about this firework display; in fact, it had been organised with all the precision of a bomb disposal unit – only we knew nothing about it. High jinks, again, at the end of a wedding. There were flashes and bangs the like of which the valley had not seen since the Earl of Pembroke's raid in 1468. There we were, sitting on the window seats of the Hall of Meredith, holding our breath until the last of the wedding guests left, and suddenly boom, bang, zing, it began. And it continued for twenty minutes – possibly the longest twenty minutes of our lives. Maybe it wouldn't have mattered had it not been the night of the Princess of Wales's funeral. Anyone who lived through that day will remember the graveside silence, the muffled sobs, the world at half mast. You could hear a pine needle drop in our valley. Anyway, there were irate phone calls, heads were shaken and the police arrived. We duly explained that 'it wasn't us, it was the wedding party', but of course the wedding party had gone home by then and we were left to carry the can. So anxious were we then to get things right, we decided to print an apology in the local paper. Huge mistake. Our simple statement: 'The owners of Gwydir Castle apologise for any inconvenience or upset caused by the discharge of fireworks on Saturday night which was done without their prior consent or knowledge,' ended up as a major news item. 'Di's Day Disrupted' ran the headline. Still, as my mother said, 'Darling, what's today's news is tomorrow's chip paper.' She was right, of course. Some small shift was taking place inside me that made me realise this. I'd noticed that the opinions of others no longer had the power to unnerve me as they had throughout my earlier life. I felt the house was bolstering my confidence, doing its best to ameliorate my past inadequacies.

The firework episode was the final straw on the evening wedding reception front. It had been an interesting experiment but nothing was worth that kind of trauma. We decided instead to keep things nice and civilised in the future: tie the knot at two, out by six. No more 'Can you find us a cab, chief?' to Peter at two in the morning. No more okey-cokey on the terrace. No more, 'We'll meet again . . .' from Uncle Ralph as he went seesawing onto the coach.

While a wedding was in motion, we kept our eyes firmly fixed on the patch of roof it would fix, the bags of lime it would buy, the old, richly perfumed roses it would plant against the walls of the Solar Tower.

17

The Room Returns and Thomas is Revealed

The panelled room returned to Gwydir on 27 July 1996. All fourteen massive crates of it were despatched from New York, then docked at Liverpool and driven in an articulated juggernaut to Gwydir. I wondered how it felt returning to the valley after all this time away. I was glad the sun was shining for it. Naturally, the juggernaut was too big for Sir Richard's bridge so it had to reverse and go the long way round, back via the wider bridge at Tal-y-Cafn. The driver of the lorry looked faintly harried on arrival. This wasn't just any old 'man with a van' outfit, as we were used to. It said 'International Art Shippers' on the side of the lorry. And the three men who piled out of the cab all wore the same blue T-shirts with logos on their collars.

The other day, I found some photographs of the room arriving at the castle. I'm wearing an old green skirt and I'm standing with my hands on my hips looking scarily like my mother, directing the traffic past the lorry on the road just outside the gates. Peter's in his shirt sleeves with his cracked old panama on, helping the men to shunt the crates across the floor of the lorry and onto the hydraulic tail that lowered them to the ground. Will and Sven were there too. Will, who had a theory about everything, was telling the men how best to take the crates off the lorry. The plan was to store the crates in the so-called Jacobean Room, the room that one day would become our library. It took five men to move one crate. They hissed through their teeth and swore in broadest Cockney when they thought I was out of earshot. I made them tea and they said, 'Blimey, you've got your work cut out with this place,' as though we hadn't noticed.

The third crate off the lorry gave us the most trouble. 'Time for the big bugger,' said the foreman. They got it off in heaves and shunts and with trapped fingers. But then it wouldn't fit through the door. It was too tall, too long, too almost everything to budge. We measured all the other doors into the house but there was no way it would fit through any of them. Only one thing for it. We would have to unpack the crate in the courtyard and carry the pieces of panelling in one by one. They set to it. I watched, every so often casting a quick glance up at the shifting cloudscape. The lid came off: our first piece of panelling, like an egg in a nest, home. We welcomed it with pats and strokes and everyone gathered round admiringly as though it were a babe in a crib. They'd been lavish with the bubble wrap – no wonder it had cost all that money to pack. You could have made a small house comfortable in it.

'Come on, lads, let's get on with it while the weather holds,' said the foreman. But the weather didn't hold. No, a dark bank of clouds was moving fast across the sky, blocking out the sun; the peacocks were heading for the underskirts of the buddleia. For such a little country Wales is a land of extremes: big views, little views; one minute bright, bright sunshine, the next it's pouring down. The weather suddenly had a fixed look on its face and it began to rain determinedly, grimly, with its head down like a charging animal, big splats of rain falling onto the dusty surface of the panelling.

'C'mon, c'mon, move it, move it,' shouted the foreman.

And move it they did. The great sheets of panelling were unpacked and unwrapped in record time and then walked in through the door to cries of 'Down, down, go on, a bit more, down.' We stood, while they unpacked, with two umbrellas aloft, trying our best to keep the rain off.

An article came out in *The Times*, Peter and I taking a full centre spread in the colour supplement; my mugshot in the fold, naturally. And suddenly it seemed like everyone had heard our story of the panelling coming back. The phone didn't stop ringing. We even did interviews for television. The first time I had a mike Sellotaped to the inside of my jumper, the thumping of my heart was so loud it drowned out my words. Inadequate words, anyway. They had to cut me from that piece. But Peter rose to the occasion; he'd found his forte in front of the camera. He'd walk casually into the shot – fingers in his jacket pockets, thumbs hanging out nonchalantly – say his piece to camera without so much as an um or an ahem, and walk off again.

But seriously, we hated the publicity. I mean really, truly hated it. Anything rather than be photographed, interviewed, spoken to. So why didn't we say 'no'? We didn't say no because we knew that if we wanted to retrieve any more of Gwydir's lost treasures we needed to get the word out to the world, quickly. So we learnt to smile sweetly, frown in a pleading way, throw our arms about a bit; and it really did pay dividends in the end. People began to telephone from all over the world. 'You don't know me, but there's a chair of yours coming up in a Christie's sale next week, says provenance Gwydir Castle . . . ' etc, etc.

And we'd buy what we could, when we could afford it. Gwydir was like a beacon with all these prodigal pieces trying to find their way back.

We stumbled across one item quite by accident while bidding for a chair – not just any old chair either, this chair had been made for Gwydir in 1666. There was a photograph of it in the 1921 sale catalogue. But, of course, some dealer had spotted it too and was running us up – early furniture with a glittering provenance was hard to come by in those days, harder still these days. With regret we had to drop out of the bidding when it reached five figures. We moped a bit about the saleroom after that, said our goodbyes to it, ran our fingers in the carved grooves of the MW for Maurice Wynn, whose chair it had been; and made unconvincing noises about 'things' not being important and said 'at least we've got our health'. And then suddenly Peter stopped mid-platitude and said, 'Oh my hat, don't look over there.' Following the course of his frozen stare, I looked over there. A fireback was leaning complacently up against the cashier's desk. We'd have known that fireback anywhere. Every piece in the 1921 sale catalogue had been scored into our memories: hadn't we spent nights and days freeze-framing each sepia image into our consciousness? That was Sir John Wynn's fireback. It had sat in the Hall of Justice year in year out, until 1921. There were his initials IW, alongside his wife Sydney's, cast in the iron, and in the centre, pride of place, the three little eagles, their wings linked together to form hearts. This fireback had been made to commemorate their marriage in 1576. Whoever had bought the MW chair must also have bought the fireback at the sale in 1921. Had the dealers missed it?

The sale was still going on in the main hall. I could hear the auctioneer drop his gavel on Lot 254. The fireback was Lot 259. We dropped our coats and ran. I'd left the bidding card in my coat pocket. Back I went, exhumed the card, flew back into the saleroom, passed the card to Peter. He threw up his hand, again, once, twice, three times, still bidding. It's ours at the drop of the gavel.

It meant we would be back on rations for the foreseeable future but at least the fireback would return with us. It felt as if Gwydir was being empowered, turned upright again like an hourglass after all these years, as though each little piece that came back was adding to the sum of the whole. And how good it was to see sand running through the old place once more.

Phase one hundred and ten: the reinstallation of the Dining Room panelling. This was by far the biggest project we'd undertaken to date. It needed careful thought. It called for clipboards, tape measures, scaled drawings; and Graham. Before any of the panelling could be walked in, we had to cleanse June's old wing with sledgehammers. We needed to knock out five rooms to create one, as it had been in Sir Richard's time. That was the fun part. Goodbye plasterboard walls, goodbye urinals and paper-thin doors you could almost put your hand through, goodbye French windows and patio doors. I couldn't muster any nostalgia for any of it even though it had served us well while we were camping in the house. We were glad to see the back of it. And what a mess we made! The dust got everywhere. In bed at night I'd find it in my mouth, like sand in sandwiches, and I'd wake up with it in the corners of my eyes as though the sandman had really been. It got through into the parts of the house that were still open to the public and people would write messages on tables to us instead of using the visitors' book.

The plasterboard partitions had been put up on the cheap in 1980-something and they came down accordingly like a pack of cards. You only had to blow on them and down they came – puff. We had a tailback of skips on the terrace which we filled with the plaster innards of each room, careful to set aside the newish timber that might come in useful for something else.

We'd co-opted extra help in the form of Caradoc (Crad for short) and Stan, both carpenters who knew their trade in the old way. They were short, stocky men with twinkles in their eyes, always joking, always acting the rear end of the pantomime horse; but so serious when the chisel was poised.

There was a long way to go before chisels could, in fact, be poised. First we had to reroof the whole wing, install new lead flashings, new cast-iron gutters, hack out and repoint the chimneys and walls, fill in where the patio doors and windows had been. By the time Will had finished stitching stone to stone with his special mortar mix, you'd never have known those excrescences had ever been. 'Belting job,' said Graham when he saw, and that really meant something, for it was hard to squeeze a compliment out of Graham. This time the roof work was done by Kenny Williams and his son Ma'in – which Peter mistook for some exotic Welsh name until he realised it was Martin with the 'rt' dropped. Syd and the Scouse Git had gone motorbike riding across the Sahara and hadn't been heard of since. Gwydir was like that. People washed into our lives and out again like the tide.

So, having cleared out all the internal partitions, we were left with one great space (as if we didn't have enough great spaces to contend with). There was a fireplace at one end with an arched mullioned window on either side, a doorway at the other end, windows down one wall, the other wall solid. At some point someone had raised the floor levels in the cellar to get better access to the barrels. We had to unpick all that, take out the floor and start again, as though none of it had ever been. Anyone who didn't know about the gaping hole into the cellar might have fallen straight in when they opened the door. It was a deep cellar and damp on account of the flooding. It was full of earth and things that wouldn't rot, like old lavatories and sheets of glass, and it smelt overwhelmingly of stale dishcloths. There was an oil tank in the middle of it, half full of oil. That was a devil to get out, but it had to be removed if the new floor was to go in two feet lower down.

A health and safety nightmare was a magnet to Will – impossible to keep him away. He loved the *frisson* of a potentially dangerous job. He volunteered to cut up the tank *in situ*. There was every likelihood that the sparks from the diamond-tipped blade would ignite the oil in the tank and blow up the house.

'You angle the sparks away from the tank, not into the

tank,' he said over the grind of the blade. 'Only someone very stupid would do that.' We stood poised with fire extinguishers. A cataract of sparks disappeared into the floor, missing the tank with only inches to spare. Our eyeballs were streaked with orange energy lines and the air was choked with petrol fumes. The silence was deafening after the grind of the blade.

'Job done,' said Will, leaning against the tank.

The work on the wing was gaining its own momentum. It was gathering speed, flattening out obstacles as they came into its path. Money always came from the most surprising sources. Just when we were down to our last bag of nails, a rebate from the Inland Revenue would arrive or a group of American tourists would appear at the door wanting a tour. We were holding our own at last and, as word spread, our visitor numbers were creeping up and up. Every week, by some miracle of faith, there was just enough to buy materials and pay the builders, but I had forgotten the last time I had bought anything new for myself. The strange thing was, there was nothing in the world I actually craved.

It was while we were working in the cellar that we came across the skeleton. With the floor removed, it was like working in an open pit of darkness. The exposed stairs took you down into it. It was cold and the walls dripped with condensation. We worked in the orange glow of hurricane lamps suspended from the wall. Peter called me over to his corner, saying he'd found something interesting. I crouched down next to him and saw what he was looking at. In the pale light I could just make out the bones lying beneath a foundation wall: a whole hoard of them, orange and brittle with age.

Someone in recent years had decided to undermine the structure of the house by digging down below the foundation level to give added height to the cellar. You could see the substructure of the soil quite clearly in cross section: the dark peaty earth nearest the top, a layer of clay, then shale, and beneath the shale were the bones. There had been a small collapse in the wall at some stage. Graham said there was likely to be an even bigger collapse if we didn't pack up the walls again sharpish. But nothing was going to make us fill up the hole again until we'd had a good look at those bones. Everyone climbed down from their respective perches on the scaffolding for a closer inspection. It wasn't as clear-cut a skeleton as you might find in an anatomy lesson. The bones were jumbled, some had almost crumbled away to dust and there was nothing very ghoulish about them. They were too old to be squeamish about. Time had sucked every last vestige of life from them, I'm glad to say, otherwise I might not have felt so compelled to rummage about among them.

We gathered round with extra torches now, the bright glow illuminating the shelf beneath the shale level where the bones lay. There was an air of conspiracy, as though we'd inadvertently stumbled upon something that was not meant for our eyes. Will, suddenly an expert in anatomy, declared that the little bone he was agitating with his trowel was surely part of a toe sequence. His theory was seconded by Kenny and before we knew where we were we had a human skeleton on our hands.

'No doubt about it.'

The only thing that was missing was the skull. A fairly crucial omission, admittedly, but that didn't stop the theories galloping on regardless, like headless horsemen. Perhaps we'd hit upon some ancient grave, given that the castle was known to have been built on the site of several very bloody battles, and these were the bones of some brave warrior. Perhaps they were the remains of the servant girl who'd been walled up by Sir John? Who knew whose they were or how long they had been there. It was strange inventing a life for these bones, that were now all but dust and forgotten shards.

We removed a handful of them from the wall and laid them on newspaper on the kitchen table. Somehow we felt we owed it to the skeleton to find out more about it: human, male, female, that kind of thing, so we could give it the appropriate send-off when the time came to fill in the wall. 'A pathologist would know,' said Peter. A pathologist, of course. Not an easy profession to come by in this part of the world. They didn't get a listing in the phone book. Martin piped up from the back of the room that the police would know. Everyone turned and looked at him in surprise. In all the time he'd worked for us, we'd never got more than a mumbled 'morning' from him. He blushed and sat down again as though exhausted by the effort.

'Bright boy, my lad,' said Kenny. Without thought we rushed to the phone and dialled the local station.

'Skeleton, you say?' said a cautious voice at the end of the line. 'In your cellar, you say?'

'Yes, yes, in our cellar.'

'And when did you find this body?'

'Day before yesterday.'

'And it's taken you this long to tell us?'

'Well, we've got part of him on the kitchen table . . . ' I stopped, thinking it best to take the conversation down another track. 'You see the bones are very old, nothing to be worried about, only we'd like to know more about them.'

'So would we,' said the sergeant sharply.

An hour later there was a screech of bicycle brakes outside the gates as Llanrwst's constabulary descended on the castle. The hole in the cellar was cordoned off with crime scene tape. The police were straight-faced, veritable portrait studies in *gravitas* – it was the time of the Fred West murders. But we couldn't keep straight faces when they started to question us. Not quite 'Where were you on the night of 27 January 1497?' but almost. They took down our dates of birth. They asked us how long we'd owned the castle, how long we'd been working on it, how we thought the bones might have got there.

'Let's not forget these are human remains, sir,' said the one who was taking down our statements in his standard issue notebook. 'It's no laughing matter.'

'But these bones are as old as Noah,' said Peter. 'Given that they're under the foundations of the house, they must be at least five hundred years old.'

The CID arrived: men in blue suits who slapped on sinister white gloves and gathered up armfuls of specimen bones from the cellar wall for examination later in the lab. The smell of aftershave and peppermint sweets mingled with the smell of rot and damp earth. With a snap of his notebook, the sergeant told us that work must stop 'until further notice'.

Meanwhile another little narrative was jogging alongside this one. Sightings of a ghost dog had been pouring in for weeks. (Those of a sceptical nature would be well advised to suspend their disbelief for a moment, hoist it up into the air and leave it dangling there until I say otherwise.) Our regular visitors kept saying, since when did we have three dogs and what a beauty the third one was. It was hound-like and pale, similar to our two but bigger, more of a wolfhound than a lurcher. It would stand very still at the far end of rooms, looking straight at you, or through you, a seemingly real dog with real fur and whiskers, and eyes as brown as conkers. But the moment you took your eyes off it, that was it: gone, as though it had never been. The three dogs were even spotted playing together in the garden. But mostly the sightings were concentrated around the area of the house where the bones had been found, as though the faithful hound had been told to sit and stay by a master who had never returned. But we hadn't seen the dog for a while, not since we'd disturbed the bones in the cellar.

Graham was getting nervous that the cellar walls were unsupported.

'What's the worst that could happen?' we asked him.

'Worst that could happen,' he said, reaching for the biscuit packet, 'is that if the gardens flood and the cellar fills up, the middle of the house might collapse.'

To our surprise, when the pathologist's report finally appeared it stated that the bones were, in fact, not human at all but were those of 'a large and ancient dog'. It was irresistible to conclude that the sightings of the dog and the bones were linked. Now we came to think of it, it was not uncommon to find animals buried beneath the foundation stones of houses. When houses like Gwydir were built, they were thought to ward away evil spirits. Chickens and cats were particular favourites, and children's shoes were also thought to be especially effective in 'shooing' away bad luck. We put the few bones we had left back in the wall, wrapped in a shroud of early snowdrops, and waved the dog off on its journey to seek its master in some other misty realm. Then Will began underpinning the foundations of the walls with sloping shelves of mortar, burying the hound for ever.

I thought no more about the bones or about the dog until another collapse at the top of the cellar steps occurred. When the rain was at its heaviest, water would run off the courtyard and seep through the wall, down the steps and into the cellar. Our next major task was to divert the water away from the house by excavating and repairing our Tudor drains. But the water had already disturbed some masonry at the base of the wall and one morning we came down to a small avalanche of tumbled stones at the top of the cellar steps. It was while we were clearing away the stones that we came across the skull. It froze us to the spot like shop-window dummies. It rolled forward theatrically, as though it wished to make our acquaintance, and came to rest at Peter's feet, perfectly white and smooth. It was a human skull – unquestionably a human skull this time – but the top of its cranium had been sliced away by a sharp surgical instrument or, dare I say it, a saw: the cut was too smooth, too precise to be otherwise. It sat and glared up at Peter, rocking slightly as though it were laughing, its eye sockets gaping like cave openings and its teeth looking like weathered tombstones below the pinched bones of its nose. Once the fright of seeing it there had subsided, it soon became like any other object – like a shell, for example, that you might pick up on a beach. We examined it closely; it was surprisingly light. It was the first skull I had ever encountered, and I think I had expected something heavier and more substantial, as if it still contained the weight of all the dreams and memories it had played host to over the years. But now it resembled a blown egg, through which matter had once passed but was now empty – a dispensed-with vessel.

I don't know why, but the name Thomas came to me as I examined the unfathomable crevices of the skull. There were no other remaining bits of bone in the wall and the inevitable questions (which have never, to this day, been satisfactorily answered) soon began to bob to the surface. Why only a head? Why had the top of the cranium been removed? Why hidden in the wall? And inevitably, did this skull have anything to do with the bones we had found in the wall but six feet away? Of course, there are no answers to these questions and never can be. Thomas now sits in Peter's room waiting to be painted, the focus of a *memento mori* amidst a crisped bunch of old roses and an hourglass.

The police have not been alerted to his whereabouts.

18
Royal Progress

We were back in a cold snap when the time came to start refitting the panelling in the Dining Room. The river had flooded three times in one month and the cellars were filled with water deep enough to swim in, should the urge have moved us. But with Will's buttressing complete, the house stood firm. Who knows where all that water went. We didn't pump it out, it just seeped gradually away between the flagstones as it had always done, leaving a floodmark around the edges of the walls like a tidemark around a bath.

It was a dark day, almost black by half past three, and the space in which we worked slightly below ground level so chilled that when we spoke speech bubbles of breath clouded upwards on the still air. Defeated eventually by the cold, I rushed off to the kitchen and cupped my hands around the boiling kettle and felt the heat percolate through my dusty mittens. When the pleasure receded and I began to burn, I opened my eyes. Leaning against the toaster was a note in Sven's near-illegible hand. It read: 'A fella phoned by the name of James Palace regardin' the prints.' There was no return number.

I stood for a long time trying to make sense of the note. During the months we had spent together, I had come to know Sven very well. I could read his moods, his highs and lows, his little dissatisfactions and his minor triumphs; I could sense how he was feeling by the tone of his voice. I knew Will, Kenny, Martin, Crad, Stan, Syd and the Scouse Git just as well. I knew how to avert a minor sulk with a small pat to the shoulder and a word of praise. I had even puzzled out the code that unlocked Sven's way of speaking, to the point where I frequently heard myself finishing off his sentences for him. A faint flicker of recognition went through my mind when I saw the note, but I couldn't dredge up how or why I knew the name James Palace. Neither did Peter and when we questioned Sven again he'd forgotten all about it. It passed quickly out of our minds too.

Practically every hour, back in the Dining Room, there was a new problem to overcome. We were faced with fourteen large crates full of bits of varnished wood, with no accompanying assembly instructions: it was like trying to follow footprints across a desert in a strong gale. We persevered. Perseverance was ever the core of our accomplishment. We had put in a working deck made out of the packing crates the panelling had been delivered in, so that we could lay out the pieces of the jigsaw. The new oak floorboards would go down last. We took tiny bites of the task in hand, slowly, patiently devouring each piece before breaking off another.

Though the panelling had originally been installed *circa* 1642, and then embellished later in the nineteenth century the wing itself dated from the mid-sixteenth century. The carved Tudor ceiling was missing from the crates, which presumably meant it had stayed with the house and burnt in the fire of 1922. We had already taken out the modern plaster ceiling which had been put up in its place. After much consultation, we had opted to put in a new coffered, plaster ceiling in keeping with the date of the panelling, compartmented into nine sections, with a heavily moulded cornice which we had specially made out of wood for the purpose. Will took to the scaffolding again and that night came down with his hair smeared in gypsum.

James Palace and his prints were not given another thought until the following morning. I was out in the garden trying to jack up an ancient vine which had fallen forwards off the wall, after a strong wind had wrenched it from its moorings. An audience of peacocks had gathered round to watch. Just as I had the vine in position, a little leaded casement opened above my head and Peter's face emerged. He shouted down excitedly: 'St James's Palace has just phoned about the prince. He wants to come and visit.' As though in answer, the peacocks let off a jubilatory honk, and I sank down among the thistles and marvelled at Sven's abysmal message-taking skills and what strange, unexpected pearls life can throw up at times.

It transpired that Prince Charles had heard about the room and had expressed a desire to see it! His private secretary had told Peter that he was visiting the area on some other business and a trip to Gwydir Castle would dovetail in quite nicely. The last time royalty had visited Gwydir was in 1899 and then they'd made a thing of it. There was bunting in the streets, brass bands and choirs. The future Queen Mary and King George V looked miserably stately in the photographs, standing outside the porch beneath a canopy of nodding roses, the princess's hands locked inside a mink muff. Commemorative trees were planted in a shady corner of the garden and given little lead plaques to prove it. Now it was our turn to make a footnote in Gwydir's history. 'A visit from royalty!' said my mother. 'Well, well. You make sure you wash your hair.'

But hair was the last thing on my mind. The panelled room was hardly finished, barely started in fact, and only four months to go before the visit. The procession of tasks was leading towards a dazzling point of crescendo. It focused our minds and gave us something to worry towards.

Once the ceiling was fully plastered, Crad and Stan ceremoniously walked in the first sheets of panelling. It sent a little shiver down the spine to see them propped up against the wall for the first time in all those years, and an even greater shiver passed through us when we discovered that the panels overshot the room by at least five inches. 'How come, Graham?' we wailed, as we pulled him in by his ear to set the mistake straight. Heads were scratched, handkerchiefs dabbed to perspiring brows, nerves pulled as taut as a high wire.

The four or five inches of pink plaster that had built up on the walls over recent years were throwing out the measurement. Every inch of plaster would have to be hacked from the walls before the panelling would fit again. We hacked it all off, marched the panelling back in and this time it did fit, with ease – and a certain satisfaction that comes when interlocking corner pieces fit snugly together. We used the wood from the packing crates to fix frames against the walls and then attached the sheets of panelling to the battens. Those packing crates were made to work for their living: not a crumb, not a shaving was lost. We'd have boiled up the bones of them for a soup had they afforded some nutritional value.

We left Crad and Stan alone once for an hour and came

back to find that the skirting boards had been put on upside down. We never left the Dining Room after that. Eighteen-hour days were commonplace but we were still weeks behind schedule. We watched over every gouge of the chisel, directed every clout of the hammer, marked the trajectory of each nail and wooden dowel. While putting in the fireplace we discovered the old stone fire surround beneath the slate hearth. It was like a reunion of long-lost siblings once we'd pieced together the various fragments. They slotted together like spoons in a canteen of cutlery, each piece fitting comfortably into the interlocking grip of its neighbour. Then the doorcase went in. We built up the ornate layers of cresting according to the 1921 photographs, affixed the mouldings, hoisted the twisted columns into place, with Crad and Stan balancing on ladders with drills poised until each crate was gradually emptied of its contents. Then came the cleaning of the panelling itself: dissolving off the wood straw which was stuck fast to the varnish; injecting each insect hole with woodworm fluid, using a tiny syringe; swiping off the dirt, waxing, polishing and coaxing the surface of each fragment of wood to a high shine again.

The crate of loose mouldings presented the biggest challenge. Each tiny piece belonged somewhere and it was up to us to find out where, and for Crad and Stan to glue and scarf and ease the pieces back into place. There were over two thousand disparate pieces to find homes for. It took two months of painstaking work to complete; and while they glued, Peter and I cleaned the many sections of leather frieze beneath the piercing glare of a halogen lamp.

An expert from the V & A came to examine the leather and deemed it highly significant, in that it had been made in London for an English market. Flanders was the usual place of origin for leather of this type, but London work crowed loudest because of its scarcity value. We were advised by those who know such things that saliva was the gentlest detergent Mother Nature had on offer, so it was out with the cotton wool swabs and (excuse the image) a fair-sized tumberful of spit which we used to circle off the grime and uncover spotlights of concentrated colour. More claret than spit, I shouldn't wonder by the end of each evening, but our own-brand cleaning solution yielded spectacular results. The gold and silver leaf beneath burst forth in an explosion of honeyed light, the geometric pattern of incised leather more intricate than we had at first imagined. It shimmered there before us, half brilliant, half clouded, like the face of a gibbous moon. Once finished, the panels of leather were hoisted up above the panelling to form the dazzling frieze that lit up the room with reflected light.

And then, finally, the floors went down. Each board of seasoned oak, some up to a width of sixteen inches, which had been specially cut for the room, was carefully selected and positioned by Peter and then fixed to the joists with cleated nails, in the old way.

Outside, we'd barely noticed that the seasons had changed. While we'd been working in the Dining Room, summer had bounced in through the gates like a carnival. Stepping out into the warm air, we breathed in those rich summer scents as though for the first time. We heard the air whistle through the wings of the wood pigeons, saw the cattle dozing in a field of buttercups beyond the garden, and ate the watercress that grew in a pool close to the Grey Mare's Tail. It was just warm enough to swim in the river. We had a favourite pool upstream that caught the sun all day, but the water came from the mountains, from the iced caverns and subterranean springs. The first plunge in was always the hardest. It was cold enough to take the words out of your mouth, but soon subsided into a warmth that numbed and flooded through your body like firewater. It washed the dust from our lungs. This water had once been clear enough to produce pearls – pearls that had been used in the Crown jewels which Sir Richard Wynn, in 1636, had presented to his queen on bended knee. In flopped the dogs, sending up a cloud of ducks from the far bank. We would lie on our backs and float in and out of the protective shadows of the great oaks, our legs caressed by the downy fingers of river weed, a crown of insects about our heads; and Peter's skin so white against the dark surface of the water because we'd been cooped up inside the house for such a long time. Afterwards, wrapped in towels, we'd drip a trail of water along the hot stones of the causeway back into the garden, where we'd walk in the shade of the giant sycamore and get sideways glances from the visiting public.

Our visitor numbers were healthier than ever now; so healthy it warranted employing a part-time gatekeeper. It was impossible to work on the panelled room and answer the door to the public. One moment the hammer would be poised over an unsuspecting nail head, next the trill of the bell would interrupt the proceedings. An argument would then ensue about who should go and answer the door. And finally, the downed hammer and the long traipse to the gate. Half an hour had vanished before you knew where you were and the countdown of days to the prince's visit had already begun to make each lost moment matter. Then in walked Heather, as if we'd conjured her out of the ether.

'I hear you need some help,' she said. I could have wept on her shoulder. She slotted straight into Gwydir like a letter in an envelope, cycling in every day from the next village down the valley, so light in spirit she might have floated away. She took charge of the gatehouse which was now let on a weekly basis to holidaymakers. She also took charge of the bed and breakfast arrangements. No more mounds of damp laundry to iron, no more eggs and bacon to cremate, marmalade to decant into little glass bowls, beds to change, baths to swill; Heather took care of it all – *takes care* of it all, in fact, for she's still with us. With the arrival of Heather we were free to concentrate our efforts on the panelled room. And as Heather walked into our lives, Sven, with regret, walked out. He had decided to go back to Liverpool to look after his mother who had become ill. He was quiet in the car as we drove him to the station. He got out onto the pavement and said a croaky 'thanks'. I suspected leaving Gwydir wasn't easy for him.

'Sven. Gwydir's always here to come back to. Remember that.'

'I will,' he said and waved goodbye without looking back.

We watched him walk down the platform steps, a

battered Adidas bag slung over his shoulder. I hoped that Gwydir had healed him of his sadness. But I would never know.

Naturally, the morning of the prince's visit we were still varnishing the Dining Room floor. It was all hell let loose in there – everyone shouting and getting in each other's way. Heather trying to buff, Stan up a ladder trying to fix a final frieze of romping cherubs to the doorcase, Peter and I attempting to apply a final coat of Danish oil to the floor, Crad fretting because he only had a funeral suit in which to meet the prince and wouldn't have time to go to Llandudno to buy himself another.

A vague programme of events had been set for the day by the prince's advisers, who had come the previous month to make sure we were what we said we were – quite what that was I can't now remember. I think they were shocked that the room he was formally due to open was not even attempting to look finished. We did our best to allay their worst fears, but they continued to phone up once a week for progress reports.

Peter was sure they'd had their eye on us for a long time prior to that. Every time you picked up the telephone receiver, a little click could be heard on the line as though someone was listening in on an extension. Orders phoned through to the local builder's merchant must ultimately have been deemed non-threatening to royal security and the clicks soon ceased.

The prince was to be dropped by helicopter onto the local rugby pitch and would then come on to Gwydir where we'd get the formalities out of the way with a line-up of local dignitaries. A tour around the outside of the house – to settle his stomach after the helicopter ride – would be followed by a line-up of the 'craftsmen', ie Will, Crad and Stan. Then a look at the room to be followed by tea and a harp recital in the Hall of Meredith, given by our friend David Watkins. The visit would end with a tree-planting session in the garden.

Just as I was about to go up and get changed (I'd exhumed an old blue dress for the occasion that had fallen off its hanger a long time ago and had ended up behind a chest of drawers – it was the best I could do), the doorbell rang. A man was standing outside the gate with the boot of his car open. A crimson handkerchief cascaded out of his jacket pocket and he wore a felt hat at a rakish angle.

'Thought you might like these,' he said without introducing himself. 'My father bought them here at the 1921 sale and I've got no use for them now. You may as well have them back.' Peter had emerged looking smart enough for both of us in a dark blue suit, and together we peered into the boot of the car where two firedogs and an iron firebasket nestled among newspapers. We recognised them immediately from the sale catalogue photographs of the Dining Room. They belonged in the fireplace where they'd sat for all those years; and now here they were, come home to roost again.

'Have them with my compliments,' he said. 'The only condition is that I can come and visit them occasionally.' We insisted that he should make his first visit now. In a little stately procession we carried them into the Dining

Room and put them back where they belonged, a firedog either side of the basket. It was uncanny. The whole ensemble of the fireplace was just as it had looked pre-1921. I wished we'd had more time to thank him. As it was, a small crowd of people was already beginning to muster at the gate in readiness for the prince's arrival.

The sprites had arrived. We'd bribed two small sons of a friend to dress up as Titania's familiars for the occasion. They wore green tights and laurel wreaths across their bare torsos and around their heads, and I gave them large bowls of cherries to distribute among the guests when the time came. Their mouths were already stained red with cherry juice, I noticed.

There was an unfortunate incident when Carw and Madoc tried to escort a sniffer dog off the premises, but by and large we managed to get everything back under control by the time the local dignitaries started arriving. There was no time now for any last-minute pruning or tidying; we just had to put on our best faces and start shaking hands. We barely recognised a soul among them. The press, television cameras, plain-clothes policemen and security guards began to flood in through the gate and soon the courtyard was awash with strangers.

Events seemed to speed up after that. One minute we heard the slice of helicopter blades overhead, the next there was a screech of brakes and a cheer rumbled through the crowd, and suddenly we found ourselves shaking hands with the Prince of Wales himself.

Mercifully, the sun was shining. He said: 'How beautiful,' when he came through the gate, and I felt so proud that after all the house had been through in recent years it was now able to enjoy this moment with its head held high.

I looked up at the windows and saw faces peering out. I remember wondering how on earth the security men had found their way up to the top of the Solar Tower. 'This happens wherever I go,' he said sadly. We wandered along the terrace with Peter giving him a potted history of the house and just as we were nearing Sir John Wynn's arch I saw a ladder disappearing behind the laurel hedge. It was Will who, only moments before, had finished mortaring the decorative sandstone finials back into place above the arch. The fountain had, of course, stopped, but no one seemed to notice, for the sunshine carried the whole proceedings forward and the vista down the avenue of clipped yew trees to the far hills was arrested by a quite spectacular circle of yellow iris which exploded out of the fountain basin. Once we'd reached the house again, I found myself telling the prince about my chilblains and he said, 'You poor thing,' which quite took the edge off my nerves. Then he asked about the ghosts. 'D'you believe in them?' he said. This was no time to tell the story of Margaret, so I just nodded which must have been rather annoying, and then Peter headed him off with stories about our other, less attention-seeking ghosts.

Then came the line-up in the Hall of Justice: Will, Crad, Stan; never had three men looked more uncomfortable in suits. Will hadn't had time to have his hair cut and his black curls fell like stage curtains against his forehead. He kept running a cement-covered finger along his collar which was making it very dirty indeed. Stan kept his eyes fixed on the floor and Crad did the talking.

'I hope my visit hasn't put you to extra trouble,' said the prince.

'Extra trouble?' said Crad. 'They've worked me like a slave to get that room finished in time,' he said, winking at me.

The Dining Room led off the Hall of Justice and no sooner had the prince caught sight of it than he was off like a greyhound out of a trap, with an 'Ah, this must be it.' As soon as he stepped over the threshold his shoes stuck fast to the floor. It held him like flypaper. The varnish we'd applied only hours before hadn't had time to dry properly and there were vast areas in the shadows that were still tacky.

We joined him so that he wouldn't feel quite so conspicuous and tried to take his mind off the floor by pointing out the highlights in the room; but really it was like trying to walk in one of those old-fashioned diving suits that have lead in the boots. He was intrigued by the room and the journey it had made in recent times, and the conversation was animated enough to make us forget about the floor in spite of the slopping noises our shoes made – similar to the sound the tide makes when it hits the harbour wall.

Then it was upstairs to the Hall of Meredith for tea. Though it was quite warm outside, a fire burnt in the grate. I'd raided our donation box to buy white china cups and saucers for the occasion. There was a throng at the tea table by the time we arrived. The Welsh cakes were going down a treat with the lord lieutenant. The sprites were under the tea table with their hands in the cherry bowl.

David began to strum on his harp and soon it was time to take our seats for the recital. We sat beneath the huge tapestry of Diana, which in a flash Peter renamed Artemis when the prince asked about it. The music began and a hush fell upon the assembled party. I wondered when a harp had last been played in this hall. Perhaps when one of Sir John Wynn's bards had last strummed a eulogy to the glories of Gwydir.

In the middle of a rather peaceful refrain the doorbell rang. I stayed confidently in my seat, not wishing to do the security men out of their one and only job of the afternoon. The music lapped on, accompanied every so often by the raucous squawk of a peacock. Then to my horror I heard the squeal of the door downstairs. A booming Germanic voice shouted up the stairs, 'Hello, hello, anyone at home?' I went cold. It was Mr and Mrs Baumgarten, the holiday-makers who had booked our gatehouse for the week. I leapt out of my chair and sped down the spiral staircase. The commotion was enough to raise the dead. 'We're here, anyone at home?' Suitcases clattered to the flagstones.

I put a finger to my lips and pointed to the ceiling.

'No, we're German,' said Mr Baumgarten, getting altogether the wrong end of the stick.

'I know you are, but please could you be quiet because we've got the Prince of Wales upstairs trying to listen to a concert.'

'Oh, that's very amusing,' he boomed. 'Ha, ha, ha.'

Eventually I got them out of the house and back into the

courtyard, but they were none too happy at being told to come back after two o'clock. The security men had obviously clocked off for their tea as the courtyard was deserted.

When I got back upstairs, everyone was just getting to their feet and it was time for the tour of the inside of the castle. We set off down the passageway which led to the Solar Tower, but the Prince kept darting on ahead saying, 'And what's in here? And where does this go?' until we'd pretty much covered every inch of the castle bar the cellars. Even the still-derelict parts of the castle had been looked in on, which he seemed to find as enthralling as we found shaming. We led him down the spiral staircase into the Solar Hall. There was a fire in here, too, and a great dripping garland of greenery strung across the fireplace. The two sprites had come in and had cast off their wreaths and become boys again. They were busy throwing cherry stones into the fire which hissed in the bed of hot ash, as though rain fell down the chimney.

The second lot of missing panelling belonged in this room, what the Victorians had called the 'Oak Parlour', Lot 65 in the sale catalogue: the room we'd assumed had not been sold and had stayed with the house and burned in the fire the following year, during Countess Tankerville's doomed ownership. It was too distressing to think of: the fine linenfold panelling and the extraordinary Caesars' fireplace, dated 1597, all gone to a fiery grave. Or had it? We'd kept the best piece for the last part of the tour.

It was while we had been reinstating the Dining Room panelling that we had come across our first clue – the first clue which told us we may have been wrong in our assumptions that the panelling had burnt. There were pieces of miscellaneous moulding that just wouldn't fit anywhere in the room, no matter what we did. And they were clearly a different colour and character from the rest. It made our task that much harder. It was like having two jigsaw puzzles all mixed up in one box. And that, as it turned out, was precisely what we'd ended up with.

One evening, just as we were clearing up for the night, Peter had casually picked a small piece of corner moulding out of one of the crates. He turned it over in his hand and a label on the back screamed, 'Lot 65 Lower Section Fireplace'.

We looked at one another disbelievingly. What could this mean? If the room had stayed with the house and burnt, how come it had been lotted up like this? And why were there bits of Lot 65 in with Lot 88? Besides which, we had often wondered why Hearst had bought one room and not the other, given that the Oak Parlour was just as important as the Dining Room. There seemed only one answer: he'd bought both rooms! Both rooms had been stripped out at the same time and some bits had become muddled up in the packaging. There was no other theory that explained away the mysterious bits of Lot 65. So the Oak Parlour may have survived to tell the tale after all!

We'd had no time to act on our findings or make any tentative searches for the lost panelling. The prince's face was a picture of quiet suspense. We'd hooked him with our quest for the second missing room and he gave the walls a thoughtful stroke as if this laying-on of hands could evoke the power of the King's Evil and magic the panelling back.

He offered to do all he could to help us find what rightly belonged to Gwydir. 'The one good thing about being a prince,' he said, 'is that people are inclined to answer your letters.'

Next, he signed the visitors' book for us. I offered him a ballpoint pen which he bestowed a pitying look upon before reaching into his inside pocket for an elegant blue fountain pen. 'With best wishes, Charles,' he wrote in a well-schooled flourish.

And then the last duty of the day was performed. We went out into the garden, narrowing our eyes against the sunshine. In keeping with tradition, a cedar of Lebanon was to be planted to commemorate the occasion. It was a scrawny thing: a snip, a bairn in comparison with its giant antecedents that stood all around, glowering down like watchful sentinels. A small group of well-wishers had gathered beyond the arch. Hazel had dug the hole in readiness and the turned sods lay in neat squares on a sheet of bubble wrap liberated from one of the crates. We'd bought a shiny new spade from Jones & Bebb for the occasion.

A soft breeze whispered through the branches of the old cedars as if to keep reminding us of their presence and their claim, also, to royal connections. It was said that Sir Richard Wynn, the second baronet, had brought them back as saplings from Madrid. He had accompanied an earlier Prince Charles (later Charles I) and the Duke of Buckingham to Madrid to woo the Spanish infanta. When they arrived in the city, they disguised themselves as gentlemen travellers from England in order to take a good look at the Spanish princess, so that the future king would still have time to slip out of a back door if he didn't like what he saw. On the first night the three got roaringly drunk and embarked on a nocturnal boating expedition that raised many a disapproving eyebrow. But somehow twelve little saplings made it back to Wales and, ironically, were planted not to commemorate the king's marriage to the Spanish infanta but to his preferred choice, the French princess Henrietta Maria, in 1625.

The chatter of small birds was all around us as Peter handed the spade to the prince. Two cabbage whites tumbled through the air; the bright iridescent eye of a shed peacock feather blinked out of the rhododendron – on the face of it, it was a day just like any other day. Except that I had the most peculiar sense of falling backwards through time as though I had slipped out of my own body and was watching the proceedings from above, as an historian might see in his mind's eye the re-enactment of a battle. We were every period in history; time was no divide. The same breeze blew through the sycamores, the same birds skimmed the edges of the clouds, the same volley of laughter filtered through the gathering in staccato bursts. All things had come together. I looked back towards the castle and saw the same view we had seen on that first day when we had stood like travellers on the threshold of our pilgrimage. But now the broken roof was fixed, the chimneys secure, the new gravel raked and the knot garden tended. And I, too, felt restored as though the house, in return, had worked its own healing magic upon me and had wiped clean all the old hurts and inadequacies.

The prince took a shovelful of rich, dark soil and poured

it onto the tangle of young roots. The little sapling would outlive us all if fate was kind to it. 'My favourite tree,' he said, handing the spade to me.

We moved back into the courtyard. Someone shouted, 'Smile for a photo, sir, would you?' and the Nikon shutter clicked on the scene as the box shutter had clicked on the same scene a hundred years ago, when the future King George V and Queen Mary had stood amidst the fallen rose petals outside the porch.

19
Reflections

*I*t is twilight, my favourite time of day, and the sun is just about to disappear behind the hill. Everything has that slightly unreal twilit tinge to it. The garden is looking impossibly beautiful. Having come down from the roof, I am now writing in the Lower Hall, the first room of the castle we came across when we trespassed all that time ago. The slug trails on the flagstones nearest the door look like silken thread discarded from some sorceress's tapestry. I sit at a long table, running down the centre of the room, which is covered with old red velvet curtains – I must remember to take the hooks out when next I have a moment. The door into the Dutch Garden is wide open and from where I sit the view of the fountain is perfectly framed. The air is busy with flying insects and the dogs lie on the lawn amid drifts of fallen cherry blossom. In the distance I hear a cow bellow, as though she is searching for a mislaid calf. If only it were possible to spear this beauty to the page, or at least keep it for a time when one really had need of it, like flowers that could be made to hold their scent right through the winter.

Peter has gone to Llanrwst to buy eggs to make an omelette for supper and I am alone in the house. I am savouring a few moments' quiet before our bed and breakfast guests arrive; a Mr and Mrs Wynn, from Ohio, who are looking forward to discussing their family tree – no wonder Peter has fled to Llanrwst!

I feel like Mariana in her moated grange: 'He cometh not, I would that I were . . .' But he will come and I am not Mariana, so you count your blessings, my girl.

It was bliss to finally recapture the house again after the upheaval of having the Prince of Wales to tea. Not that I didn't enjoy it. I did. It's just that if there's a choice between front of house and backstage, I'm the sort who'd plump for backstage every time. We kept the house closed for two days afterwards. We had the place completely to ourselves because the German tenants had left early under a cloud lined with recriminations. They said that they hadn't been offered a drink on arrival; that the slates rattled in the wind; that the peacocks kept them awake at night; that the gatehouse was badly appointed and didn't have any egg spoons. I tried to explain that a drink was merely a courtesy not a prerequisite of their stay with us; I tried to explain that the gatehouse had a flat lead roof; that the peacocks were as much a part of Gwydir as the garden that surrounded it. I tried to . . . I'm still at a loss to know what an egg spoon is.

We had a letter from them a few days later. It said: 'staying in your gatehouse for more than one day is a special kind of punishment'. I have noticed that it is much easier not to feel resentment when one is happy. Luckily, I was feeling happy the morning we received that letter, so we burnt it ceremonially on the fire while offering up a few simple Anglo-Saxon profanities, and left it at that. We've become better at dealing with crises now. More tolerant, less apt to fly off the parapet when people dare to criticise the house. We used to take it all so personally: criticise the house and you'd cut us to the quick. And I'd snarl back as though I were a she-lion protecting her young, or her old, more like. There were people who got the point of it and people who didn't, and there were some people (and this was an eye-opener, I can tell you) who were eaten up with petty resentments and jealousies, who saw our dream fulfilment as a mirror to their own failures. They'd say things like, 'I could easily have bought this house but my wife thought it was too dark inside. How do you cope living here?' But for every one of those, there were five hundred who wished us well. More than enough to replenish my faith in human nature.

We must be doing something right because only last month we won an award for our bed and breakfast accommodation. We thought it was a joke at first, but no, they sent us a flashy trophy with 'Best Travel Secret of the Year', inscribed upon it. To be fair, we had made a big effort to smooth out the inconsistencies. The bats were offered alternative accommodation and so forth, and the result now elicits a 'wow' from our guests on entering the bedrooms instead of the 'oh' of past occasions. The bedrooms are warm and rather *gemütlich*, if I say so myself: lashings of hot water; breakfast served upstairs to the rustle of fine linen in a room we have now panelled. (I knew the panelling we had stored in my mother's garage would one day come into its own.) I suspect the award is an indication of how far we've come since the days when doves nested on the lintels and frogs lived in the corridor outside the kitchen. But in pursuit of the summit we only have eyes for the climb ahead and not all the smaller peaks already conquered.

We still live with buckets in certain parts of the house, hence Peter and I running around in pyjamas at the beginning of this account, but with select use of locked doors and private signs we are able to exclude people from those areas still requiring attention. Nothing much has changed in our own quarters. Our clothes still hang from broom handles across the windows; we've suffered seven outbreaks of dry rot in one corner of our bedroom and the walls now resemble an abstract patchwork of different plastering interventions. I suspect we will be the last to benefit from the current phase of renovations. Still, if we want a really comfortable night we are now able to book ourselves into the King's Room on the other side of the house.

It still gives us a shock to go into the Dining Room each morning and see all that polished splendour unravelled before us – a bit like it must be to look in the mirror after a facelift. Who knows when the last dinner party was thrown in there. It might be my imagination but sometimes, late at night, when I go in to close the shutters, I swear you can smell cigar smoke, as though the ladies have just left the room and the gents are swapping a lewd story or two over the port and Havanas. At night, when the chandelier and the candles in the mirrored sconces are lit, the room comes alive. The panelling glows like the surface of a glazed fruitcake.

As far as the Oak Parlour goes, the prince has been as good as his word. He wrote letters to the Hearst family asking if they knew the whereabouts of a panelled room which belonged, by rights, to a certain castle in Wales. But until this morning no information had been forthcoming. Today, however, we had a breakthrough. Quite coincidentally, we received a letter from a lady in Yorkshire, a relative of whom had owned the castle around the time of the sale. She said that she had discovered the auctioneer's copy of the sale catalogue, 'annotated with prices, etc', in her great-uncle's effects and also some further correspondence relating to the sale in 1921. In the margin against the Oak Parlour, was written: 'Sold with Lot 88.' This is our first bit of hard evidence that actually confirms Lot 65 was taken from the house before the fire! Now we know it has survived and must exist somewhere in the world. She ends her letter by saying if we would like more information, to contact her again. Tomorrow, with beating hearts, we shall write to her and the fuse of another adventure will be lit.

Endings always put me in an inventorising mood – that notion of taking stock of one's life. But this is not an ending: for us, it is more of a beginning. Every day here is the beginning of something; the slow turning of a page that leads to another and another . . .

Only yesterday someone asked me if we had any regrets about taking on the restoration of such a big house. I said 'Regrets?' because the question had never occurred to me before, in spite of the fourteen-hour days, the cold and the chronic chilblains. How could we possibly have any regrets about trying to restore a house that has shown us so much of life. A house that has given us friends, memories and adventures: opened doors into different time zones, cradled us both in the arms of its cool interiors; and made our love inviolate by forging it from the black depths of Margaret's legacy. We always knew it, but now we are certain: *amor vincit omnia.* In our case, love *has* conquered all.

Peter has just come in, his hand shielding a candle on a pewter plate, his face in heavy chiaroscuro. He kisses the top of my head and presents me with a bar of my favourite chocolate. Wait, I will ask him the same question.

'Regrets?' he asks dubiously. He takes my hand and leads me to the door. The edges of the clouds are trimmed with white light from the setting sun. The trees on the far hillside have retreated into deep, deep shadow. The air is as soft and warm tonight as the breath of swallows. The falling sun is behind the fountain now: the spring of water is a shaft of gold setting light to the entire garden. There's no need for words. The garden is bursting with the expectation of spring. It is all hope and promise, and there is the thrill of another chase ahead. We're on the trail of the second room. We're pecking at crumbs again. We're building castles in the air.

ALSO AVAILABLE IN EBURY PRESS PAPERBACK

HISTORICAL BIOGRAPHY

Green Gold *Alan and Iris Macfarlane*
£6.99   (ISBN: 0091895456)   ☐
Forgotten Voices of the Great War *Max Arthur*
£7.99   (ISBN: 0091888875)   ☐
The Birdman *Isabella Tree*
£7.99   (ISBN: 0091895790)   ☐
The Toy Maker *Anthony McReavy*
£7.99   (ISBN: 0091895812)   ☐

TRAVEL WRITING

French Leave *John Burton Race*
£6.99   (ISBN: 0091898307)   ☐
A Foreign Affair *Shaun Briley*
£6.99   (ISBN: 0091896703)   ☐
The Angel Tree *Alex Dingwall-Main*
£6.99   (ISBN: 0091895472)   ☐
Tick Bite Fever *David Bennun*
£7.99   (ISBN: 0091897432)   ☐

HOW TO ORDER
FREE POST AND PACKING
Overseas customers allow £2.00 per paperback

BY PHONE: 01624 677237

BY POST: Random House Books, C/o Bookpost, PO Box 29, Douglas, Isle of Man, IM99 1BQ

BY FAX: 01624 670923

BY EMAIL: bookshop@enterprise.net

Cheques (payable to Bookpost) and credit cards accepted

Prices and availability subject to change without notice.
Allow 28 days for delivery.
When placing your order, please mention if you do not wish to receive any additional information.

www.randomhouse.co.uk